Childbirth

Other Books of Related Interest:

Opposing Viewpoints Series

Adoption

Family

Reproductive Technologies

At Issue Series

Should Parents Be Allowed to Choose the Gender of
Their Children?

Contemporary Issues Companion

Women's Health

Current Controversies Series

Teenage Pregnancy and Parenting

"Congress shall make
no law . . . abridging
the freedom of speech,
or of the press."

First Amendment to the U.S. Constitution

The basic foundation of our democracy is the First Amendment guarantee of freedom of expression. The Opposing Viewpoints Series is dedicated to the concept of this basic freedom and the idea that it is more important to practice it than to enshrine it.

OPPOSING VIEWPOINTS® SERIES

▌Childbirth

Christina Fisanick, Book Editor

GREENHAVEN PRESS
A part of Gale, Cengage Learning

GALE
CENGAGE Learning™

Detroit • New York • San Francisco • New Haven, Conn • Waterville, Maine • London

Christine Nasso, *Publisher*
Elizabeth Des Chenes, *Managing Editor*

© 2009 Greenhaven Press, a part of Gale, Cengage Learning.

Gale and Greenhaven Press are registered trademarks used herein under license.

For more information, contact:
Greenhaven Press
27500 Drake Rd.
Farmington Hills, MI 48331-3535
Or you can visit our Internet site at gale.cengage.com

For product information and technology assistance, contact us at

Gale Customer Support, 1-800-877-4253
For permission to use material from this text or product, submit all requests online at www.cengage.com/permissions

Further permissions questions can be emailed to permissionrequest@cengage.com

Articles in Greenhaven Press anthologies are often edited for length to meet page requirements. In addition, original titles of these works are changed to clearly present the main thesis and to explicitly indicate the author's opinion. Every effort is made to ensure that Greenhaven Press accurately reflects the original intent of the authors. Every effort has been made to trace the owners of copyrighted material.

Cover photograph reproduced by permission of iStock.

LIBRARY OF CONGRESS CATALOGING-IN-PUBLICATION DATA

Childbirth / Christina Fisanick, book editor.
    p. cm. -- (Opposing viewpoints)
    Includes bibliographical references and index.
    ISBN-13: 978-0-7377-4196-4 (hardcover)
    ISBN-13: 978-0-7377-4197-1 (pbk.)
    1. Childbirth. I. Fisanick, Christina.
    RG651.C55 2009
    618.2--dc22

                                                2008032947

Printed in the United States of America
1 2 3 4 5 6 7 12 11 10 09 08

Contents

Chapter 3: How Can Rights and Preferences Be Honored During Childbirth?

Chapter 4: Who Should Assist and Be Present During Childbirth?

Why Consider Opposing Viewpoints?

> *"The only way in which a human being can make some approach to knowing the whole of a subject is by hearing what can be said about it by persons of every variety of opinion and studying all modes in which it can be looked at by every character of mind. No wise man ever acquired his wisdom in any mode but this."*
>
> John Stuart Mill

In our media-intensive culture it is not difficult to find differing opinions. Thousands of newspapers and magazines and dozens of radio and television talk shows resound with differing points of view. The difficulty lies in deciding which opinion to agree with and which "experts" seem the most credible. The more inundated we become with differing opinions and claims, the more essential it is to hone critical reading and thinking skills to evaluate these ideas. Opposing Viewpoints books address this problem directly by presenting stimulating debates that can be used to enhance and teach these skills. The varied opinions contained in each book examine many different aspects of a single issue. While examining these conveniently edited opposing views, readers can develop critical thinking skills such as the ability to compare and contrast authors' credibility, facts, argumentation styles, use of persuasive techniques, and other stylistic tools. In short, the Opposing Viewpoints Series is an ideal way to attain the higher-level thinking and reading skills so essential in a culture of diverse and contradictory opinions.

In addition to providing a tool for critical thinking, Opposing Viewpoints books challenge readers to question their own strongly held opinions and assumptions. Most people form their opinions on the basis of upbringing, peer pressure, and personal, cultural, or professional bias. By reading carefully balanced opposing views, readers must directly confront new ideas as well as the opinions of those with whom they disagree. This is not to simplistically argue that everyone who reads opposing views will—or should—change his or her opinion. Instead, the series enhances readers' understanding of their own views by encouraging confrontation with opposing ideas. Careful examination of others' views can lead to the readers' understanding of the logical inconsistencies in their own opinions, perspective on why they hold an opinion, and the consideration of the possibility that their opinion requires further evaluation.

Evaluating Other Opinions

To ensure that this type of examination occurs, Opposing Viewpoints books present all types of opinions. Prominent spokespeople on different sides of each issue as well as well-known professionals from many disciplines challenge the reader. An additional goal of the series is to provide a forum for other, less known, or even unpopular viewpoints. The opinion of an ordinary person who has had to make the decision to cut off life support from a terminally ill relative, for example, may be just as valuable and provide just as much insight as a medical ethicist's professional opinion. The editors have two additional purposes in including these less known views. One, the editors encourage readers to respect others' opinions—even when not enhanced by professional credibility. It is only by reading or listening to and objectively evaluating others' ideas that one can determine whether they are worthy of consideration. Two, the inclusion of such viewpoints encourages the important critical thinking skill of objectively evaluating an author's credentials and bias. This evaluation will illuminate an author's reasons for taking a particular stance on an issue and will aid in readers' evaluation of the author's ideas.

It is our hope that these books will give readers a deeper understanding of the issues debated and an appreciation of the complexity of even seemingly simple issues when good and honest people disagree. This awareness is particularly important in a democratic society such as ours in which people enter into public debate to determine the common good. Those with whom one disagrees should not be regarded as enemies but rather as people whose views deserve careful examination and may shed light on one's own.

Thomas Jefferson once said that "difference of opinion leads to inquiry, and inquiry to truth." Jefferson, a broadly educated man, argued that "if a nation expects to be ignorant and free . . . it expects what never was and never will be." As individuals and as a nation, it is imperative that we consider the opinions of others and examine them with skill and discernment. The Opposing Viewpoints Series is intended to help readers achieve this goal.

David L. Bender and Bruno Leone,
Founders

Introduction

"For women in industrialized countries, the lifetime risk of death from pregnancy complications is 1 in 2,800, but that risk for women worldwide is 1 in 74."

Family Health International

In an age in which many formerly fatal diseases have been all but eradicated, it may seem surprising that nearly 530,000 women worldwide died during childbirth or soon after in 2005. The number comes from *Make Every Mother and Child Count*, a report released by the World Health Organization (WHO), and it is not expected to decline in the near future. The WHO attributes many of these maternal deaths to inadequately funded health care systems and lack of sufficient medical knowledge by prenatal and postpartum caregivers. It would be easy to assume that all of these deaths, most of which were preventable, occurred in non-Western countries, yet according to a 2007 report released by the National Center for Health Statistics; the maternal death rate in the United States is higher than it has been in decades. The causes of and potential solutions to these alarming findings are far from simple.

Accurately calculating maternal death has long been a challenge for researchers due in part to inaccurate or missing birth and death records. Simply determining a definition for maternal death has proven to be extremely difficult. The WHO originally defined maternal mortality as "the death of a woman while pregnant or within 42 days of termination of pregnancy, irrespective of the duration and site of the pregnancy, from any cause related to or aggravated by the pregnancy or its management but not from accidental or incidental causes." In

2000, they expanded the definition to include "late maternal death, which is defined as the death of a woman from direct or indirect obstetric causes more than 42 days but less than one year after termination of pregnancy." Skeptics of the WHO's 2005 figures have argued that the expansion of this definition explains the high maternal death rate. The WHO defends its data by acknowledging the need to include late maternal death in its calculations in order to accurately assess the situation and to find a possible solution.

The WHO report uncovered several causes behind worldwide maternal deaths: bleeding/hemorrhage (25 percent), infections (13 percent), unsafe abortions (13 percent), eclampsia (12 percent), obstructed labor (8 percent), other direct causes (8 percent), and indirect causes (20 percent), including such pregnancy complications as malaria, anemia, HIV/AIDS, and cardiovascular disease. Some researchers focus on the rise of cesarean sections and obesity as the main culprits for the increase in U.S. maternal deaths, which have spiked to 12 out of every 100,000 births. Although this rate is far lower than many other countries, especially developing nations, researchers are nonetheless concerned given that the current maternal death rate in the United States is higher that it has been since 1977.

Although these data reveal the diagnosable causes of maternal deaths, some researchers argue that the reasons for high fatality rates are tied much closer to social attitudes about women and childbirth. According to lawyer and women's advocate Anika Rahman, "In most low-income countries, pregnancy and childbirth are the leading causes of women's death and disability." She attributes this fact to societal views about women, noting that women in these nations are often forced to bear children before they are physically capable of doing so safely and that they have little access to proper medical information and services. Other researchers take a different approach. For example, the online childbirth organization Birthing Naturally argues that "our lifestyle has a strong impact on our pregnancy outcomes. Good nutrition, adequate exercise and a safe environment can prevent many of the problems with pregnancy and childbirth." Those lifestyle modifications might be feasible for most women in developed nations like the United States, but in countries where poverty leads to a lack of nutritious foods and unsafe living conditions, such changes seem almost impossible.

Even though researchers are aware of some of the causes of maternal deaths, finding adequate solutions is another matter entirely. Raising the overall quality of life in poor nations would be an ideal place to start, but most childbirth advocates acknowledge the difficulty and complexity of such a mission. Rahman argues that wealthy nations such as the United States should contribute more funds to world health programs, such as the United Nations Population Fund, which is the largest international organization dedicated to women's health. The International Development Committee, a British-based legislative group, agrees with Rahman. In a March 2008 meeting, they noted that there has been little progress in reducing world maternal deaths in the past twenty years. They concluded that "a key factor in this collective failure has been insufficient political will to drive actions to improve the health of women, both at the international and national levels." Ultimately, the WHO argues that the only way to reduce the rate of maternal deaths is to ensure worldwide access to high quality healthcare before, during, and after pregnancy.

Given that childbirth can be a dangerous undertaking no matter where in the world it is attempted, it is no wonder there are so many divergent views on the issues surrounding how it can be done safely and with the best interests of the mother and child in mind. The authors in *Opposing Viewpoints: Childbirth* debate current views on childbirth in the following chapters: How Can Safety and Comfort During Childbirth Be Assured? What Are the Best Conditions for

Childbirth? How Can Rights and Preferences Be Honored During Childbirth? and Who Should Assist and Be Present During Childbirth? Despite the varying approaches to issues related to childbirth, finding tenable solutions to reducing maternal mortality rates will continue to be a goal of many health organizations around the globe.

OPPOSING
VIEWPOINTS®
SERIES

CHAPTER 1

How Can Safety and Comfort During Childbirth Be Assured?

Chapter Preface

For most of human history, women were encouraged to eat and drink during labor. It was believed that women needed their strength and that eating and drinking would prevent fatigue and even nausea. All of that changed in the 1940s when a small study was published that showed that women who ate and drank during labor were more likely to aspirate food into their lungs while under general anesthetic. Although the study was limited and the anesthetics used in labor are much different today than they were over sixty years ago, women are still often prohibited from eating and drinking during labor.

The risks of aspiration are great and dangerous outcomes can include pneumonia or even death. Given the potential for harm, health care providers usually seek to limit the possibility for such complications by requiring that women not eat or drink during labor. Although some doctors have become more lax about allowing women to eat and drink during early labor, it remains commonplace for laboring women to be restricted to hard candies and ice chips throughout most of their labor. According to Brigham and Women's Hospital in Massachusetts, women undergoing uncomplicated labor should consume only clear liquids and no solid food for up to eight hours before going into labor. That way, should they need general anesthesia for an emergency cesarean section, the risks of difficulties will be lower. Hospitals across the country echo this standard.

In recent years, however, women and some health care providers have begun to reconsider this restrictive practice. According to childbirth educator Kathy Peterson, the possibility of a woman needing general anesthesia during childbirth is 1 in 33,000. In addition, modern anesthetic practices, when done properly; nearly eliminate the risks of aspiration. Furthermore, Hence Gore, author of *The Thinking Woman's Guide to Better Birth*, argues that a pregnant woman's stomach is never entirely empty no matter how much time has passed since she consumed food or drink. Also, recent studies have shown that women who are given light food and drink during labor have much shorter labor than women whose food and liquid intake is more restricted.

Health care providers want to ensure that women have safe and comfortable childbirths, and certainly, no woman would want to put herself or her baby in danger. Such concerns have led many women and their physicians to limit the risks of eating and drinking during labor by using IVs and antacids to keep women hydrated and to break down any food that is consumed. As the viewpoints included in the following chapter, this issue is one that will continue to be debated given the potentially serious risks.

"Early placement of an epidural . . . does not increase the length of labor, or the likelihood of women ending up with a cesarean delivery."

Epidurals Are Safe for the Management of Pain During Childbirth

Kathryn J. Alexander

In the following viewpoint, Kathryn J. Alexander, coauthor of Easy Labor: Every Woman's Guide to Choosing Less Pain and More Joy During Childbirth, *argues that epidurals have been proven safe as a method of managing the pains of labor and delivery. Therefore, she notes, women should not be discouraged or ashamed to request them during childbirth. She further counters the claims of natural, or drug-free, childbirth advocates by describing her own difficult labor and delivery experience that was significantly eased by the administration of an epidural.*

As you read, consider the following questions:

1. How many women each year receive an epidural during childbirth, as cited by Kathryn J. Alexander?

Kathryn J. Alexander, "Insufferable," *Babble*, 2007. www.babble.com. Copyright © Kathryn J. Alexander and Nerve Media. Reproduced by permission.

2. By how much, does Alexander report, has labor induction increased since1989?

3. How are women who choose pain relief such as epidurals monitored during labor and delivery, according to the author?

At the final meeting of my childbirth preparation course, the instructor finally broached the subject of labor pain relief. It was a topic that, up until that point, had not been discussed with much gusto. Even then, in the eleventh hour of the class, all I heard were words like "trust," "empowerment" and "self-confidence." Was this a scout meeting? Trust, empowerment and self-confidence are not anesthetics.

I was pregnant for the first time at 37. Having coped with Motrin-defying menstrual cramps since adolescence, I felt I had a reasonable pain threshold. But as my due date approached, I grew increasingly concerned about the physical experience that awaited me. I wanted more concrete information about how painful childbirth would be. I kept hearing a response from my caregivers that was vague and patronizing: "Childbirth is different for everyone."

Surely they were kidding? After several thousand years of women bringing forth life, that's *all* we know about the experience? Is it really so different for everyone that no general body of knowledge exists that could tell me more explicitly how much pain I was *most likely* going to experience? I honestly wanted to know. Generally speaking? For most women?

My good friend Maureen, a nurse jaded by years of treating patients in pain, reluctantly gave in to my plea to describe exactly how labor felt. She told me that until she was given an epidural, her labor felt like "a living hell." Darkly, she repeated "a living hell," then caught herself and said, "I hope that doesn't scare you." Noooo, don't be silly.

Labor Pain as Good Pain

Meanwhile, my birthing teacher and all the books I'd picked up (including the popular *Easing Your Labor*, by Adrienne Lieberman, and the ubiquitous *Natural Childbirth The Bradley Way*, which came out in 1984 and was revised in 1996) insisted labor pain was "good pain." In the chapter titled "The Myth of the Painless Birth," Lieberman attempts to persuade her pregnant readers that "the experience of pain may actually help you to feel a deeper pleasure." She concludes, "with adequate preparation for childbirth, you can give up the self-indulgent and disappointing fantasy that your labor should be painless and replace it with a more realistic and ultimately more rewarding commitment to working *with* your pain." (italics hers)

This claim by the experts that women become better people, possibly even better mothers, for having successfully given birth without the benefit of medical pain relief, led me to wonder what excruciating physical challenge my husband should triumph over to become a superior father—and would I get to choose?

Even before my own difficult labor, the attempt to reframe the pain of childbirth as "good pain" struck me as a bit of a sham. I found myself wondering why my teachers were talking about good pain rather than good pain *relief*. What had been overlooked was how to deal with the type of pain I would rather live (and birth) without, and that was: *any type* of pain. I was skeptical that the distinction between pains would still be important to me when my uterus began contracting.

Marci Lobel, Ph.D., director of the Stony Brook Pregnancy Project at Stony Brook University, says, "Popular books written for pregnant women may overstate the effectiveness of childbirth preparation in reducing pain." Glossing over the severity and intensity of labor pain, and emphasizing the use of non-medical forms of pain management such as breathing and relaxation techniques (the cornerstone of most childbirth preparation methods) leads women to underestimate the pain involved in childbirth, and to overestimate their own ability to cope with it without the help of modern medicine.

In the early 1980s, a Canadian researcher, Dr. Ronald Melzack, and his team from McGill University, conducted studies that attempted to measure the pain level of women in labor. Using a pain-measurement scale called the McGill Pain Questionnaire (MPQ) to assess the nature and intensity of labor pain in first-time mothers, the researchers found that labor pain was rated as "severe" by 30 percent of the mothers, and 38 percent of the group rated their labor pain as "very severe." Add to this the 28 percent of laboring first-time mothers who chose the words "horrible" or "excruciating" to describe their pain, and you begin to understand why euphemisms are popular among childbirth professionals.

More than 2.5 million of the 4 million of us who give birth each year in the U.S. opt for an epidural, so why was it assumed in my class that the goal was to attempt to cope with as much pain as possible for as long as possible, rather than to eliminate the pain *as soon as possible*, through the use of modern medicine? I was puzzled by the fact that, at the world-renowned teaching hospital where I was to give birth, modern medicine was presented merely as a backup to non-medical techniques.

Epidurals: Conflicting Research

In my class, I was warned that an anesthesiologist might not be immediately available, or that some physicians were concerned with possible risks that may be associated with early placement of an epidural; specifically, the risks of increase in length of labor, or increased likelihood of a cesarean delivery. This concern, I was told, may lead to my having to wait hours until my cervix was sufficiently dilated to the magic number of 4 to 5 centimeters before I would be considered "ready" for an epidural. These potential glitches in my ability to receive timely relief sounded ominous to me, but the casual tone of the instructor's precautionary statements suggested that the possibility of my having to endure extreme pain for a period of time was seen as a reasonable part of any woman's birth experience.

Recent research had concluded that early placement of an epidural—or epidural on demand—does not increase the length of labor, or the likelihood of women ending up with a cesarean delivery. At Chicago's Northwestern University, Pam England tells pregnant women that birth is an "adventure." Cynthia Wong, M.D., and her colleagues, studied the effects of the timing of epidurals on over 700 first-time moms in a landmark study, published in 2005 in the *New England Journal of Medicine*. Half of the women received narcotic pain relief injections, but not epidurals, until they were more than 4 centimeters dilated. The other half received the epidural much earlier in labor. The study concluded that there was no difference in the incidence of cesarean deliveries among the early versus later group. In fact, the women who received the earlier epidurals actually had a shorter labor—on average 90 minutes shorter—than those who were given the epidural at 4 centimeters. Commenting on this study in an editorial published in the *New England Journal of Medicine*, Dr. William Camann, director of Obstetric Anesthesia at Boston's Brigham and Women's Hospital and associate professor of anesthesia at Harvard Medical School, said, ". . . safe and effective pain relief . . . should not be withheld simply because an arbitrary degree of cervical dilation has not yet been achieved." Even the American College of Obstetricians and Gynecologists (ACOG) says, in an official bulletin issued in 2006, "Recent studies have shown that epidural analgesia does not increase the risks of cesarean delivery. The fear of unnecessary cesarean delivery should not influence the method of pain relief that women can choose during labor."

Mothers Rated Epidurals Most Effective for Labor Pain Relief					
		Effectiveness of Specified Method			
	% Using Technique	Very Helpful	Somewhat Helpful	Not Very Helpful	Not Helpful At All
Epidural	63%	78%	15%	3%	4%
Breathing Techniques	61%	21%	48%	21%	10%
Position Changes/ Movement	60%	19%	60%	16%	5%
Hands-On Techniques	32%	30%	52%	13%	6%
Mental Strategies	30%	22%	52%	18%	7%
Narcotics	30%	24%	42%	20%	9%

Note: Based on a survey of 1,583 mothers who gave birth within 24 months of the survey, conducted May 15 to June 16, 2002.

TAKEN FROM: Maternity Center Association, Harris Interactive.

In spite of this, many popular childbirth professionals suggest women should "try" to labor and give birth without medication—and that we should *want* to.

A Basic Human Instinct

In her wildly popular book titled *Birthing From Within*, Pam England tells pregnant women that birth is an "adventure" and states that "many childbirth teachers and healthcare professionals unwittingly have misguided mothers by reinforcing the hope that pain can be avoided, and by supporting our natural childlike tendency to look outward for comfort and relief." She goes on to warn us that "... adopting a passive stance to dealing with pain has its consequences," and asks, "Is the reassuring option of analgesics or an epidural keeping you from plumbing the depth of your own resources?"

Not only is the book used widely by childbirth professionals throughout the country, the concept has become a phenomenon. England has courses, workshops and a girl shop on her Web site, where shoppers can find CDs, videos, "birth art" and other items, including tiny tee shirts for the newborn, emblazoned with the words "My Mama's a Birth Warrior."

Childbirth professionals with a nature-worshipping bias against medical pain relief seem to suggest that only self-indulgent, entitled control freaks—void of spirituality, feminist enlightenment and the ability to bond with their young—would want a pain-free birth. But the wish to avoid pain is not an upper-middle-class whim. It's a basic human instinct, one that has been useful in preserving our species. Since when did childbirth become about having a transformative personal experience rather than about getting a healthy baby and not dying (or wishing you were dead) in the process?

Taking Control of Childbirth

Well, starting in the mid-1960s. At that time, women began to revolt against depersonalized maternity care characterized by the routine use of pain relief that rendered women unconscious or close to it. By rejecting these medications, women hoped to take back control of their birth experience. Birth philosophies that promoted the use of breathing and relaxation techniques, such as Lamaze and the Bradley Method, took hold as *the* way to achieve a rewarding birth experience.

In the 1980s, women who enjoyed more social, political and economic power than any previous generation decided breathing techniques (and painful birth) were not for everyone, and the newest pain relief method, the epidural, began to replace natural birth for most American women. During this time, roughly 22 percent of American women used an epidural during childbirth. By 1992, that rate more than doubled. Today, on many busy maternity units, 80 to 90 percent of women choose an epidural for pain relief. According to a recent study in the journal *Anesthesiology*, only 6 percent of women in large hospitals and 12 percent in small hospitals opted for drug-free births.

In other words, there is a significant gap between how women are *prepared* to give birth by childbirth professionals and how women *choose* to give birth once they reach the delivery room. It seems that the more women choose medication, the more vocal becomes the anti-medical movement. The more popular epidurals become, the louder grows the voice insisting women are passing up an opportunity for personal growth and spiritual enrichment.

It's hard to deny that birth is over-medicalized. Our nation's C-section rate is 30 percent and rising. Labor induction (artificially starting labor before it begins on its own) has doubled since 1989. And I don't care how much of your hospital's budget was spent revamping their maternity unit to look like your favorite small luxury hotel, just try to help yourself to something in the fridge when you feel hungry during labor; you will quickly be reminded you are in an institution.

But pain relief is not the culprit. These are *care* issues that have to do with how physicians practice, how legal threats loom and how big institutions can't seem to deliver comfort— even with pretty new wallpaper and lots of big pillows.

Honoring Choice

Contrary to the suggestion made by its opponents, the epidural is not an unnecessary medical intervention that deprives women of satisfaction and empowerment while giving birth. Moreover, telling pregnant women they should attempt to deal with their pain as an exercise in "plumbing the depths of their inner resources," rather than honoring their choice to give birth on their own terms, *without pain*, is in itself disempowering.

It is true that if you want an epidural, or a narcotic drip, or any other form of medical pain relief during labor, you will wind up hooked up to a lot of wires: most likely an IV, a Foley catheter and two belts around your waist—one to monitor the baby, one to monitor your contractions. Your blood pressure may dip. You may feel itchy. You may spike a fever.

But here is the great big On The Other Hand: *You will not be experiencing mind-blowing pain.*

Ultimately, I found Maureen's description of childbirth as "living hell" to be similar to my own (only when I describe it, I use more expletives). I walked, squatted, used hydrotherapy and massage, but labor was an agony that wrenched my body for hours until I was finally "ready" for the relief provided, almost instantly, by an epidural. It was not until the torture ended that I was able to connect with the joy and excitement of knowing I was about to finally meet my daughter.

I don't doubt that, for some women, natural childbirth provides an emotional boost that is powerful and gratifying. But for me, giving birth was the fulfillment of a lifelong wish to have a baby, not a means of self-actualization. The real adventure began when I became a parent.

| "Epidurals are associated with major disruptions in the process of birth."

Epidurals During Labor Are Not Safe for the Mother and Baby

Sarah J. Buckley

Sarah J. Buckley is an Australian physician and the author of Gentle Mothering: The Wisdom and Science of Gentle Choices in Pregnancy, Birth, and Parenting. *In the following viewpoint, she argues that epidurals can be dangerous for mothers and babies. In addition, epidurals can slow the process of labor, which can lead to a cesarean section or the use of instruments like forceps, which can increase the risk of complications. While Buckley acknowledges that epidurals provide effective pain relief during labor and delivery, many women report that they do not increase feelings of satisfaction after childbirth.*

As you read, consider the following questions:

1. What does the author assert was the percentage of U.S. women given epidurals during childbirth in 2002?

2. What are the possible side effects of instrumental delivery on newborns that Buckley reports?

Sarah J. Buckley, "The Hidden Risks of Epidurals," *Mothering*, vol. 133, November–December 2005, pp. 50–58. Reproduced by permission of the author.

3. For what percentage of women is an epidural inadequate pain relief, according to the viewpoint?

The first recorded use of an epidural was in 1885, when New York neurologist J. Leonard Corning injected cocaine into the back of a patient suffering from "spinal weakness and seminal incontinence." More than a century later, epidurals have become the most popular method of analgesia, or pain relief, in US birth rooms. In 2002, almost two-thirds of laboring women, including 59 percent of women who had a vaginal birth, reported that they were administered an epidural. In Canada in 2001–2002, around half of women who birthed vaginally used an epidural, and in the UK in 2003–2004, 21 percent of women had an epidural before or during delivery.

Epidurals involve the injection of a local anesthetic drug (derived from cocaine) into the epidural space—the space around (epi) the tough coverings (dura) that protect the spinal cord. A conventional epidural will numb or block both the sensory and motor nerves as they exit from the spinal cord, giving very effective pain relief for labor but making the recipient unable to move the lower part of her body. In the last five to ten years, epidurals have been developed with lower concentrations of local anesthetic drugs, and with combinations of local anesthetic and opiate painkillers (drugs similar to morphine and hesperidins) to reduce the motor block. They produce a so-called walking epidural.

Spinal analgesia has also been increasingly used in labor to reduce the motor block. Spinals involve drugs injected right through the dura and into the spinal (intrathecal) space, and they produce only short-term analgesia. To prolong the pain-relieving effect for labor, epidurals are now being coadministered with spinals, as a combined spinal epidural (CSE).

Epidurals and spinals offer laboring women the most effective form of pain relief available, and women who have used these analgesics rate their satisfaction with pain relief as very high. However, satisfaction with pain relief does not equate with overall satisfaction with birth, and epidurals are associated with major disruptions to the process of birth. These disruptions can interfere with a woman's ultimate enjoyment of and satisfaction with her labor experience, and they may also compromise the safety of birth for the mother and baby. . . .

Effects on the Process of Labor

Epidurals slow labor, possibly through the above effects on the laboring woman's oxytocin release, although there is also evidence from animal research that the local anesthetics used in epidurals may inhibit contractions by directly affecting the muscle of the uterus.

On average, the first stage of labor is 26 minutes longer in women who use an epidural, and the second, pushing stage is 15 minutes longer. Loss of the final oxytocin peak probably also contributes to the doubled risk of an instrumental delivery—vacuum or forceps—for women who use an epidural, although other mechanisms may be involved.

For example, an epidural also numbs the laboring woman's pelvic floor muscles, which are important in guiding her baby's head into a good position for birth. When an epidural is in place, the baby is four times more likely to be persistently posterior (POP, or face up) in the final stages of labor—13 percent compared to 3 percent for women without an epidural, according to one study. A POP position decreases the chance of a spontaneous vaginal delivery (SVD): in one study, only 26 percent of first-time mothers (and 57 percent of experienced mothers) with POP babies experienced an SVD: the remaining mothers had an instrumental birth (forceps or vacuum) or a cesarean.

Anesthetists have hoped that a low-dose or combined spinal epidural would reduce the chances of an instrumental delivery, but the improvement seems to be modest. In one study, the Comparative Obstetric Mobile Epidural Trial (COMET), 37 percent of women with a conventional epidural experienced instrument births, compared with 29 percent of women using low-dose epidurals and 28 percent of women using combined spinal epidurals.

For the baby, instrumental delivery can increase the short-term risks of bruising, facial injury, displacement of the skull bones, and cephalohematoma (blood clot under the scalp). The risk of intracranial hemorrhage (bleeding inside the brain) was increased in one study by more than four times for babies born by forceps compared to those with spontaneous births, although two studies showed no detectable developmental differences for forceps-born children at five years old. Another study showed that when women with an epidural had a forceps delivery, the force used by the clinician to deliver the baby was almost twice the force used when an epidural was not in place.

Epidurals also increase the need for Pitocin to augment labor, probably due to the negative effect on the laboring woman's own release of oxytocin. Women laboring with an epidural in place are almost three times more likely to be administered Pitocin. The combination of epidurals and Pitocin, both of which can cause abnormalities in the fetal heart rate (FHR) that indicate fetal distress, markedly increases the risk of operative delivery (forceps, vacuum, or cesarean delivery). In one Australian survey, about half of first-time mothers who were administered both an epidural and Pitocin had an operative delivery.

The impact of epidurals on the risk of cesarean is contentious; differing recent reviews suggest no increased risk and an increase in risk of 50 percent. The risk is probably most significant for women having an epidural with their first baby.

Note that the studies used to arrive at these conclusions are mostly randomized controlled trials in which the women who agree to participate are randomly assigned to either epidural or no epidural pain relief. Nonepidural pain relief usually involves the administration of opiates such as hesperidins (aka pethidine). Many of the studies are flawed from high rates of crossover—women who were assigned to nonepidurals but who ultimately did have epidurals, and vice versa. Also, noting that there are no true controls—that is, women who are not using any form of pain relief—these studies cannot tell us anything about the impact of epidurals compared to birth without analgesic drugs. . . .

Maternal Side Effects

The most common side effect of epidurals is a drop in blood pressure. This effect is almost universal and is usually preempted by administering IV fluids before placing an epidural. Even with this "preloading," episodes of significant low blood pressure (hypotension) occur for up to half of all women laboring with an epidural, especially in the minutes following the administration of a drug bolus. Hypotension can cause complications ranging from feeling faint to cardiac arrest and can also affect the baby's blood supply (see below). Hypotension can be treated with more IV fluids and, if severe, with injections of epinephrine (adrenaline).

Other common side effects of epidurals include inability to pass urine (necessitating a urinary catheter) for up to two-thirds of women, itching of the skin (pruritus) for up to two-thirds of women administered an opiate drug via epidural; shivering for up to one in three women, sedation for around one in five women, and nausea and vomiting for one in twenty women.

Epidurals can also cause a rise in temperature in laboring women. Fever over 100.4° F (38° C) during labor is five times more likely overall for women using an epidural: this rise in temperature is more common in women having their first babies, and more marked with prolonged exposure to epidurals. For example, in one study, 7 percent of first time mothers laboring with an epidural were feverish after 6 hours, increasing to 36 percent after 18 hours. Maternal fever can have a significant effect on the baby (see below).

Opiate drugs, especially administered as spinals, can cause unexpected breathing difficulties for the mother, which may come on hours after birth and may progress to respiratory arrest. One author comments, "Respiratory depression remains one of the most feared and least predictable complications of . . . intrathecal (spinal) opioids."

Many observational studies have found an association between epidural use and bleeding after birth (postpartum hemorrhage). For example, a large UK study found that women were twice as likely to experience postpartum hemorrhaging when they used an epidural in labor. This statistic may be related to the increase in instrumental births and perineal trauma (causing bleeding), or may reflect some of the hormonal disruptions mentioned above.

An epidural gives inadequate pain relief for 10 to 15 percent of women, and the epidural catheter needs to be reinserted in about 5 percent. For around 1 percent of women, the epidural needle punctures the dura (dural tap); this usually causes a severe headache that can last up to six weeks, but can usually be treated by an injection into the epidural space.

More serious side effects are rare. If epidural drugs are inadvertently injected into the bloodstream, local anesthetics can cause toxic effects such as slurred speech, drowsiness, and, at high doses, convulsions. This error occurs in around one in 2,800 epidural insertions. Overall, life-threatening reactions occur for around one in 4,000 women. Death associated with an obstetric epidural is very rare, but it can be caused by cardiac or respiratory arrest, or by an epidural abscess that develops days or weeks afterward.

Later complications include weakness and numbness in 4 to 18 per 10,000 women. Most of these complications resolve spontaneously within three months. Longer term or perma-

Cesarean Rates Around the World

The World Health Organization's guidelines suggest that a country's rate of cesarean section should lie somewhere between 10 and 15 percent of all deliveries.

Country	Year	C-section rate
Austria	2003	22.1%
Brazil	2003	30–70%
Canada	2002	22.5%
Chile	2002	30.7%
Denmark	2003	19.1%
England	2002–03	22%
Guatemala	2002	11.4%
Honduras	2001	7.9%
Netherlands	2002	13.5%
Peru	2000	12.9%
Sweden	2002	16.4%
Taiwan	2007	33%
Turkey	2001	30%
United States	2005	30.2%
Wales	2001–02	24.4%

TAKEN FROM: Sarah Buckley, "The Hidden Risks of Epidurals," *Mothering*, vol. 133, November–December, 2005.

nent problems can arise from damage to a nerve during epidural placement: from abscess or hematoma (blood clot), which can compress the spinal cord; and from toxic reactions in the covering of the spinal cord, which can lead to paraplegia.

Side Effects for the Baby

Some of the most significant and well-documented side effects for the unborn baby (fetus) and newborn derive from effects on the mother. These include, as mentioned above, effects on her hormonal orchestration, blood pressure, and temperature regulation. As well, drug levels in the fetus and newborn may be even higher than in the mother, which may cause direct toxic effects. For example, epidurals can cause changes in the fetal heart rate (FHR) that indicate that the unborn baby is lacking blood and oxygen. This effect is well known to occur soon after the administration of an epidural (usually within the first 30 minutes), can last for 20 minutes, and is particularly likely following the use of opiate drugs administered via epidural and spinal. Most of these changes in FHR will resolve themselves spontaneously with a change in position. More rarely, they may require drug treatment. More severe changes, and the fetal distress they reflect, may require an urgent cesarean.

Note also that the use of opiate drugs for labor analgesia can also cause FHR abnormalities. This process makes the real effects of epidurals on FHR hard to assess because, in almost all randomized trials, epidurals are compared with meperidine or other opiate drugs.

One researcher notes that the supine position (lying on the back) may contribute significantly to hypotension and FHR abnormalities when an epidural is in place. Another found that the supine position (plus epidural) was associated with a significant decrease in the oxygen supply to the baby's brain (fetal cerebral oxygenation).

The baby can also be affected by an epidural-induced rise in the laboring mother's temperature. In one large study of first-time mothers, babies born to febrile (feverish) mothers, 97 percent of whom had received epidurals, were more likely than babies born to afebrile mothers to be in poor condition (low Apgar score); have poor tone; require resuscitation (11.5 percent versus 3 percent); or have seizures in the newborn period. One researcher noted a tenfold increase in risk of newborn encephalopathy (signs of brain damage) in babies born to febrile mothers.

Maternal fever in labor can also directly cause problems for the newborn. Because fever can be a sign of infection involving the uterus, babies born to febrile mothers are almost always evaluated for infection (sepsis). Sepsis evaluation involves prolonged separation from the mother, admission to special care, invasive tests, and, most likely, administration of antibiotics until test results are available. In one study of first-time mothers, 34 percent of epidural babies were given a sepsis evaluation compared to 9.8 percent of nonepidural babies.

Drugs and Toxicity

Every drug that the mother receives in labor will pass through the placenta to her baby, who is more vulnerable to toxic effects. The maximum effects are likely to be at birth and in the hours immediately after, when drug levels are highest.

There are few studies of the condition of epidural babies at birth, and almost all of these compare babies born after epidurals with babies born after exposure to opiate drugs, which are known to cause drowsiness and difficulty with breathing. These studies show little difference between epidural and nonepidural (usually opiate-exposed) babies in terms of Apgar score and umbilical-cord pH, both of which reflect a baby's condition at birth. However, a large-population survey from Sweden found that use of an epidural was significantly associated with a low Apgar score at birth. . . .

It is important to note that a newborn baby's ability to process and excrete drugs is much less than an adult's. For example, the half-life (time to reduce drug blood levels by half) for the local anesthetic bupivacaine (Marcaine) is 8.1 hours in the newborn, compared to 2.7 hours in the mother. Also, drug blood levels may not accurately reflect in the baby's toxic load because drugs may be taken up from the blood and stored in newborn tissues such as the brain and liver, from where they are more slowly released. . . .

Satisfaction with Birth

Obstetric care providers have assumed that control of pain is the foremost concern of laboring women and that effective pain relief will ensure a positive birth experience. In fact, there is evidence that the opposite may be true. Several studies have shown that women who use no labor medication are the most satisfied with their birth experience at the time, at six weeks, and at one year after the birth. In a UK survey of 1,000 women, those who had used epidurals reported the highest levels of pain relief but the lowest levels of satisfaction with the birth, probably because of the highest rates of intervention.

Finally, it is noteworthy that caregiver preferences may, to a large extent, dictate the use of epidurals and other medical procedures for laboring women. One study found that women under the care of family physicians with a low mean use of epidurals were less likely to receive monitoring and Pitocin, to deliver by cesarean, and to have their babies admitted to newborn special care.

Epidurals have possible benefits but also significant risks for the laboring mother and her baby. These risks are well documented in the medical literature but may not be disclosed to the laboring woman. Women who wish to avoid the use of epidurals are advised to choose caregivers and models of care that promote, support, and understand the principles and practice of natural and undisturbed birth.

> "[An episiotomy] is actually a helpful procedure, along with the other unnatural aspects of labor and delivery."

Episiotomies Are Sometimes Prudent

Gerard M. DiLeo

Gerard M. DiLeo is a board-certified obstetrician-gynecologist and author of The Anxious Parent's Guide to Pregnancy. *In the following viewpoint, he asserts that most doctors would prefer not to perform an episiotomy, but some circumstances, such as baby size and position, require the procedure for the safety of the mother and the baby. DiLeo notes that doctors can reduce the risks of episiotomy complications by choosing the best location, type of cut, suture material, and repair technique. Ultimately, he recommends that women allow their physicians to make the final decision whether or not to cut.*

As you read, consider the following questions:

1. What are some reasons the author gives for deep tearing during childbirth that the author gives?
2. As listed by DiLeo, what are the three main types of suture used in episiotomy?
3. What are pick-ups with teeth, according to DiLeo?

Gerard M. DiLeo, "Episiotomy," GynOb.com. Reproduced by permission.

Episiotomy is a procedure as unnatural as any elective surgery. Most folks, to be sure, prefer not to be cut for any reason. But just because it's unnatural doesn't mean it's unjustified. An episiotomy involves making a vertical incision in the tissue between the floor of the vagina and the rectum, thereby increasing the circumference of the exit for the baby's head at the time of delivery. It is painless when done under an epidural, local anesthetic, or pudendal (nerve) block. The circle of tissue that is the outlet for the baby is made larger and the chance of tearing less.

Since it is easier to repair a surgical incision than a traumatic tear, the decision to cut an episiotomy is made at the last moment when it looks like there may be tearing without one. In this way, it should be looked at as preventative. But it only prevents superficial tears. No episiotomy—no increase in diameter of just the outlet—will prevent deep tears if the force of the delivery (due to a large head, forceps, or precipitous expulsion) exceeds the elasticity of the tissues of the pelvis. Something will have to give, and it's usually the baby's head that wins.

Some espouse never cutting an episiotomy. Although this philosophy won't cause deep tears, the superficial ones can increase the time of recovery by a few weeks. The gamble here, of course, is whether or not a patient will get away with nothing needing repair. It is tempting, but it is certain that a surgical repair of a straight incision hurts less and heals better than a disarray of tissue split in several different directions.

What's the best approach? Leave it up to your obstetrician—that's why you chose your doctor. Of course, discuss the issue ahead of time so that both of you are clear on a common plan. But keep in mind that your doctor doesn't do episiotomies if clearly not needed. They're included in the global fee, so there's no financial incentive, and it's more work to repair one than not repair one. So if it looks like the baby will deliver without unreasonable stretching and risk, your doctor will gladly skip the episiotomy. If it looks as if there may be some trauma, an episiotomy—the smallest necessary—will be used for your benefit.

Absorbable suture means you don't need the stitches removed. And because of the unique immunology of the area, infection is rare. The area ultimately heals well, even when there was tearing. In fact, it' s often difficult to tell a woman' s had one by exam. Thinning of the floor of the vagina is from the passage of the baby, not from the decision to do an episiotomy or not. One must remember that childbirth is an amazing phenomenon of physics, pushing a body's capacity to the max. Compared to the actual delivery, episiotomy can be thought of as an inconvenience or an advantage, depending on what could have happened with or without it. But it is a secondary consideration when an irresistible force—the baby—meets an immovable object—you.

Future Chances of Tearing

All an episiotomy does is prevent the superficial tears. Deeper tears are usually the result of a large baby or if the skin of the perineum isn't given enough time to slowly elasticize (as with pushing in Stage II of labor). Shortened Stage II's occur with precipitous deliveries or with forceps (usually in emergency situations). The vacuum extractor usually doesn't yield enough outward force to pull a baby over the increased resistance of non-elasticized tissue. (It'll pop off first—a safety feature).

With episiotomy, the midline method is the preferable method to me, because the tissue is thinner there—therefore, less tissue trauma, less bulk to heal, less pain. The downside is that if it extends with a large baby, it'll tear right into the rectum. This can be fixed right there, though. The alternative is a right or left "mediolateral" episiotomy, in which the cut is made from the center of the floor of the vagina down an angle, on either side of the rectum. This will spare the rectum . . . maybe. . . . but a tear will shred in many planes much

Circumstances that Require an Episiotomy

An episiotomy may be needed for any one or more of the following reasons:

Birth is imminent and your perineum hasn't had time to stretch slowly

Your baby's head is too large for your vaginal opening

Your baby is in distress

You need a forceps or vacuum assisted delivery

Your baby is in a breech presentation and there is a complication during delivery

You aren't able to control your pushing

"Episiotomy,"
American Pregnancy Association, March 2006.

thicker tissue than the midline would have. It's a mess. A midline is much easier to recover from than a mediolateral. And a midline with an extension tear into the rectum is easier to recover from than a mediolateral with extension tears along irregular paths into all of that thicker lateral tissue.

If you've had a previously bad tear, the chances of the same thing happening are less, since the tissues of the vagina and perineum have already been "elasticized" once. But that's in a perfect world, where it's assumed that all other parameters are the same—same doctor, same type of episiotomy, same size and position of baby, same type of labor, etc. No two pregnancies are alike, however, so I'm afraid it's going to be "I don't know." Generally, the more babies one has, the less likely the prudence (notice I didn't say necessity) of an episiotomy.

Do know this: most obstetricians—myself included—love to get by without an episiotomy at all. But I'm not afraid to cut one if I can see it's the only thing holding the head back without nasty tearing—It's a last second call. But in my practice, I cut no "automatic" episiotomies.

It would be a good idea to discuss with your doctor the policy on episiotomy—are they automatic, are they midline or mediolateral . . . and why? Are they with quickly dissolving suture or delayed-absorbing suture, etc.?

Suture Used in Episiotomy

There are three main types of suture used in episiotomy:

Quickly dissolving—usually chromic, which dissolves in about two weeks and usually softens during this time.

Delayed dissolving—usually a "polyglycolic," which dissolves over about six to eight weeks, or longer, but can stiffen and give a sticking sensation sometimes.

Permanent suture—used when there is an infection and previous episiotomy repair breakdowns. I don't use this. So far, anyway.

Technique for Episiotomy Repair

I was taught how to repair an episiotomy by a nurse midwife when I was in medical school. Many doctors use a tissue forceps called "pick-ups with teeth." This is nothing more than a pair of tweezers with two teeth on one shaft interdigitating with a single tooth on the other one. This sandwiching pincer grasp is very efficient in picking up the tissue so that the necessary tension is provided against which to drive a curved needle.

Back at Charity Hospital in New Orleans, where I trained, there were wards . . . where there would be twelve patients at a time. During "postpartum" rounds, I began to notice that my patients had less episiotomy pain than those of other doctors. Over the years, I've discovered what I think is the reason: I don't use pick-ups with teeth.

I use my index finger and thumb to gently support the tissue I'm sewing. In other words, I use no instruments except the actual needle holder. With pick-ups with teeth, every time tissue is grasped, because of the design of the forceps, there are three little holes placed into the tissue grasped. In my opinion, a series of three-holes along the repair route become pockets of inflammation in the recovery period, increasing the pain associated with episiotomy repair. We're talking about perhaps fifty to sixty little holes. True, these pose absolutely no danger, but I feel they hurt more until they heal within a few days.

I use what's called the "modified" midline episiotomy. In this technique, I perform a midline, but then a make a little right angle cut on either side of the lowest part of the cut, which then skirts the circular musculature that surrounds the rectum. In this technique, a smaller episiotomy is needed, and this eliminates the higher risk of any tears through the rectum. . . .

I don't cut episiotomies automatically.

I hate them. Unless the patient needs one. Then I love them, because if I have cut one, I'm averting big, bad tears that are much worse than an episiotomy would be.

Episiotomy and Future Problems

The literature has continually pursued whether cutting episiotomies or not cutting them contributes to future problems with *urinary incontinence*, "fallen" bladders, prolapse of the uterus in later years, and rectal weakness. After exhaustive studies and lengthy follow-up of patients in groups having and not having episiotomies, the current thinking is that episiotomy (done or not done) does not contribute to or cause these problems.

The direct cause of these problems depends on how many babies have been delivered, how many large babies have been delivered, age, gravity, and other predisposing factors that deteriorate tissue integrity, like alcoholism, diabetes, and smoking.

"Just because episiotomy was once routine doesn't mean it still should be."

Episiotomies Are Not Necessary

Beth Howard

In the following viewpoint, Beth Howard, author of Mind Your Body: A Sexual Health and Wellness Guide for Women, *argues that episiotomies are often not needed and can lead to complications, including difficult healing and possible infection. Even though episiotomy rates have gone down in recent years, some doctors continue to perform them routinely without consideration of each woman's needs at delivery. She recommends that women discuss the issue with their health care providers and try their best to avoid unnecessary episiotomies by following a healthy diet and regularly massaging their perinea before and during labor and delivery.*

As you read, consider the following questions:

1. According to Howard, by what percentage does an episiotomy increase women's risk of third- and fourth-degree lacerations?

2. What is the current rate of episiotomies in the United States, as cited by the author?

3. How does Beth Howard define perineal massage?

Susan Spears figured she was on her way to a smooth delivery—after seven hours of active labor, this first-time mom felt ready to push her baby out. But just 20 minutes later, and against her expressed wishes, her doctor decided to move things along by performing an episiotomy, an incision in the perineum—the space between the vagina and rectum. In an instant, a healthy 7-pound, 11-ounce girl was born.

Spears was thrilled to have her daughter in her arms, but her recovery, thanks to the episiotomy, was less than thrilling. Within a day of delivery, the stitches her doctor had put in to sew up the cut dried out (she hadn't been instructed on how to care for them, such as taking frequent sitz baths—soaking in a shallow bath of water—to keep them moist). They pulled painfully, and some even ripped out. "It hurt whenever I moved or even laughed," she says. Even after the site had ostensibly healed, Spears "felt" the incision—and grew skeptical about the necessity for the procedure. "I believe my doctor did an episiotomy because she was trying to hurry along the birth process," she says.

Fast-forward seven years. Pregnant with a second daughter, Spears switched to a practitioner who assured her she'd do everything possible to avoid an episiotomy. During labor, "she massaged my perineum," says Spears. "I popped out a 9-pound baby after about 20 minutes of pushing without so much as a tear." The lesson? It pays to question some birthing practices. Just because episiotomy was once routine doesn't mean it still should be. Lots of moms are left to wonder if their episiotomies were necessary. Some experts are also asking questions.

Your Mom Certainly Had One

It wasn't until giving birth in hospitals became the norm, starting in the 1920s, that episiotomies took hold. Women frequently tore during delivery, and making a preemptive cut was considered kinder—a way to prevent pain and protect moms from problems blamed on childbirth, such as incontinence and sexual dysfunction. Doctors were trained to do one with nearly every birth, and it became a standard of care by the 1950s.

But when researchers finally got around to scrutinizing the common wisdom by the 1970s and 1980s, study after study showed that routine episiotomies do not lessen pain or prevent urinary or anal incontinence or sexual problems—and that sometimes they actually cause rectal problems and increase pain. "Episiotomy does more harm than good," says Katherine Hartmann, M.D., Ph.D., director of the Center for Women's Health Research at the University of North Carolina in Chapel Hill, which reviewed four decades' worth of data on episiotomy for the *Journal of the American Medical Association.*

Studies show that women who get episiotomies have the same rates of infection, healing, and pelvic pain, and they may resume sex later. They also have a greater risk for damage to the anal sphincter, which can cause lifelong bowel incontinence. An episiotomy increases a woman's risk of third- and fourth-degree lacerations by 13 percent. (A third-degree tear goes through the anal sphincter; a fourth-degree goes all the way into the rectal muscle.)

In fact, some doctors now believe that episiotomies promote further injury by providing a starting place for more serious tears. "I had an episiotomy, but I still ended up being torn from my vagina to my rectum," says Sonja Angell of Jasper, Georgia, who gave birth to an 8-pound, 9-ounce girl two years ago. "So what was the point?" Most U.S. women have a midline episiotomy, which is cut straight down and is more likely to cause a serious tear than those cut at an angle.

But Your Daughter Probably Shouldn't

Thankfully, the tide is turning against episiotomy. The American College of Obstetricians and Gynecologists (ACOG) has denounced routine episiotomy, and medical schools have done a 180. The rates of episiotomy are dropping as newly minted OBs start their careers. Twenty years ago, more than 80 percent of births involved the unkind cut—today it's just one in three.

Yet, as many as a million women still get unnecessary episiotomies every year. Old habits die hard—especially when it comes to medical practices, says Dr. Hartmann. If you'd rather not be surprised by a scalpel, your best bet is to stay informed, and talk to your doctor or midwife. Follow these steps, from pregnancy through delivery day.

Avoiding an Episiotomy

Educate yourself. Know when episiotomy is necessary. An incision is the right course when the fetus is in trouble and a quick delivery is critical, or when instruments such as forceps or a vacuum will be used. Your provider may also tell you she'll consider an episiotomy if your baby is very premature. "A preemie's skull is softer than that of a full-term baby, and the pressure of the mother's perineum on the baby's head can trigger bleeding in the brain," says Michelle Collins, a certified nurse-midwife at Vanderbilt University in Nashville, Tennessee.

Bring up the subject. Ask your provider what his episiotomy rate is and under what circumstances he generally performs one. The rate should ideally be less than the target rate of 15 percent, Hartmann says.

Don't think it's too early to ask. You certainly don't want to wait until you're on the delivery table to bring it up. If your doc hasn't kept up on the latest info about episiotomies, he may be routinely performing them—unless his patients pipe up. "Right from the beginning we told my OB that I didn't want an episiotomy if at all possible," says new mom Lindsey Coffman of Springfield, Missouri. "When she came in the

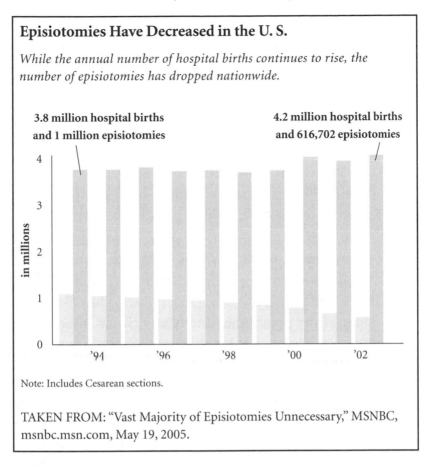

Episiotomies Have Decreased in the U. S.

While the annual number of hospital births continues to rise, the number of episiotomies has dropped nationwide.

3.8 million hospital births and 1 million episiotomies

4.2 million hospital births and 616,702 episiotomies

Note: Includes Cesarean sections.

TAKEN FROM: "Vast Majority of Episiotomies Unnecessary," MSNBC, msnbc.msn.com, May 19, 2005.

room to deliver my daughter, she remembered. I didn't tear or get cut." Coffman was lucky; about two-thirds of first-timers *do* have some tearing.

Pay attention to good pregnancy nutrition. Eating healthily may actually help you avoid an episiotomy. "Proper nutrition aids in the formation of healthy skin and perineal tissue, and that helps the perineum's ability to be more flexible and stretch well," says Collins. A good diet also helps keep a mom's weight gain to a normal limit, which in turn helps to keep the baby's weight within a healthy range. That increases the chances that labor will progress normally and hopefully not require an incision.

Perineal Massage

Take matters into your own hands. Perineal massage, or "working" the skin of the perineum to make it more supple and elastic in late pregnancy, may help decrease both tears and the need for an episiotomy, says Vani Dandolu, M.D., director of urogynecology and pelvic reconstructive surgery at Temple University School of Medicine in Philadelphia. One study found that 24 percent of women in first pregnancies who performed prenatal perinea massage had no tears, compared with just 15 percent of those who didn't practice the technique.

The key is to do it regularly in the final months of pregnancy. Here's how: Apply a lubricant (K-Y Jelly, vitamin E, cocoa butter) around the perineum. Then place your thumbs about 1 1/2 inches inside your vagina, pressing downward and to the sides at the same time. Gently stretch for several minutes, until you feel a slight burning or stinging sensation. Hold the pressure for about two minutes or until the tissue begins to feel slightly numb. Massage the lower vagina with your thumbs for several more minutes, remembering to avoid the urinary opening. This technique should take between five and ten minutes, and be performed once or twice a day starting at about the 34th week of pregnancy. Perineal massage may not be advisable for some women, such as those with active herpes lesions, so talk to your provider first.

"My husband massaged my perineum with vitamin E for many a night during pregnancy," says Dawn Opie of Alexandria, Virginia. "I'm pretty certain that was the clincher in my avoiding an episiotomy."

Clarify Your Wishes

Reiterate your wishes. You've discussed and agreed on it before, but at the time of delivery, be sure to remind your doctor that you want to avoid an episiotomy. "It can also help to let the labor nurse know, too," says Jay Goldberg, M.D., clinical associate professor in the department of obstetrics and gynecology at Jefferson Medical College in Philadelphia.

Deena Taylor, a New York City mother of three, is glad her nurse was on board at her first delivery. "We had talked to the doctor ahead of time. He didn't seem to think episiotomy was a big deal," she says. But her labor nurse made the difference: "She kept urging me to push, did perineal massage, and challenged me to prove my doctor wrong; he was sure I'd need an episiotomy because of the baby's size. He was shocked when the nurse called him to deliver."

Be willing to take it slow. If you are giving birth with the help of a midwife, she may know this by training and instinct: Carefully controlling (as best you can!) your pushing in the second stage of labor gives the perineum time to stretch naturally. Dr. Goldberg promotes a technique he calls "super crowning." "At the time of crowning, rather than let the baby's head burst through uncontrollably, you hold it steady or even push it in slightly for a couple of contractions to allow the tissues to stretch slowly and naturally," Dr. Goldberg says. He believes this approach significantly reduces the incidence of vaginal lacerations—especially third- and fourth-degree tears. Of course, no woman can rule out the possibility that interventions like episiotomy may become necessary, and complications do happen, despite good intentions. But by knowing the facts and discussing them with your provider, you might be able to avoid an episiotomy. "When I got pregnant the second time, I knew the questions to ask: 'What percentage of your births involve episiotomy?' and 'What do you do to avoid it?'" Spears says. "As a result, it was a great experience. Having done it both ways, there was no question what was best for me."

| "Caesareans have saved more lives than almost any other surgical procedure in history."

Cesarean Deliveries Are Safe and Frequently Necessary

Tiffanie Darke

In the following viewpoint, novelist and writer Tiffanie Darke defends cesarean sections as necessary medical procedures. She notes that women who have cesareans, whether by choice or out of necessity, are often chastised by others for being failures. Drawing on her own childbirth experience, she argues that women whose babies are born by cesarean section are anything but weak. After all, many women who have cesarean deliveries do so after long, difficult labors and then must recover from major surgery. Darke concludes that cesarean sections should be credited for saving the lives of women and babies.

As you read, consider the following questions:

1. As of February 2007, what is the cesarean rate in Britain?

2. According to the author, the latest rise in cesarean rates can be attributed to what factor?

3. How many of all induced pregnancies, as reported by Darke, end in cesarean sections?

[February 2007's] announcement that the caesarean rate in Britain has now risen to one in four births, was met with predictable reactions. There was much gnashing of teeth from the midwife quarter, the inevitable mutterings about "too posh to push" and all those hairy-faced ladies from the National Childbirth Trust leapt up to blame the doctors for forcing women into unnatural childbirth. Honestly, these days you'd think the act of having a baby was political. How you choose to deliver your child seems to say more about you than your social class, income or choice of handbag.

You never hear it for caesareans. They are the underclass of childbirth options. Women who have caesareans are treated like failures, or soft, pain-dodging cop outs. Never mind that the latest rise in caesareans has actually been among emergency, not elective procedures, which means that these women will have tried very hard to give birth naturally, or that a caesareans major abdominal surgery, leaving you incapacitated for weeks.

What is routinely ignored however, is that caesareans have saved more lives than almost any other surgical procedure in history. Natural childbirth is hugely complicated: the large brain of the baby human is required to pass through the tiny, fixed pelvis of its mother. Hemorrhaging, infection and obstruction of labor are all frequent obstacles to safe birth and in the past, childbirth has been the biggest killer of women. Not any more. But unlike the Pill, the vote or equal pay, or any of those breakthroughs which have given women control over their lives and their bodies, the caesarean is consistently denigrated.

Attempting Natural Birth

My own story illustrates the point. Expecting my first child at the end of October [2006], I hopped right on to the natural childbirth wagon. Egged on by magazines, yoga classes, birthing "gurus" and all manner of new age propaganda, my preparation for the big event was all about my own personal female empowerment. I would travel to the astral portal of all feminine life, tripping on the beauty of my contractions, and see the meaning of life through the haze of my pain as I welcomed my baby to the world.

Such was my indoctrination that I believed the strongest painkiller I would need was my husband's ability to hypnotize me. I wasn't even allowed to use the word pain. Contractions? No—they're surges, dear.

There's nothing wrong with this approach, of course, plenty of women do manage to birth their children with comparative ease. But it is by no means true for all of us. I remember one friend telling me "the problem with childbirth is no one tells you how painful it is", and she's right. But then I thought, how difficult could it be if women the world over did it once, twice, even several times?

Aromatherapy candles at the ready, my due date came and went. As did the next two weeks, as I heaved my groaning body up and down Parliament Hill in north London in a bid to "bounce the baby down". At one point two well-spoken women stopped me to palm a Buddhist chant they assured me would get the baby out. What is this collusion?

At my scan, I begged the doctor not to set a date for my induction. Sympathetically he agreed as I was in good health, and I embarked on round after round of acupuncture, reflexology and any sort of hocus pocus that professed to bring on labor. I could have gone for a week's stay in the Portland [Hotel] for the amount I spent on alternative treatments.

Inducing Labor

But by November 7, there was still no sign of movement so at 8:30 A.M. my husband and I turned up at hospital for the induction. Little did I know then that half of all inductions end

Indications for C-section

There are many reasons for doing a C-section:

- Herpes infection could expose the baby to serious illness, and since this virus can be caught by exposure of the baby to the virus in your birth canal, C-section will theoretically (not guaranteed) avoid exposure.

- A previous C-section with a vertical scar on the uterus (womb) may pose a danger of uterine rupture with a labor. This type of incision is considered to heal more weakly. . . .

- Breech delivery is another problem addressed by C-section. The only allowable vaginal delivery with a breech (any non-head-first—"vertex"—position) is the frank breech, when both legs are flexed straight up (not bent at the knees), such that the buttocks will make an effective dilating "wedge" and the ankle won't jam against the exit (as when the knees are flexed). . . .

- Failure to progress, defined as lack of descent of the baby's head or lack of dilation of your cervix for two hours in active labor, or for three hours in active labor with an epidural. . . .

- Fetal distress obligates an obstetrician to C-section if a vaginal delivery is not imminent. The standard of care is such that a hospital is expected to put together a C-section within 30 minutes, so if vaginal delivery can happen before that, it just might beat out the C-section approach. . . .

- Serious bleeding from an abnormally placed or separating placenta elevates C-section to a heroic, lifesaving procedure . . .

"Cesarian Delivery," www.gynob.com.

in emergency caesareans, mainly because chemically induced labor is stronger, longer and harder and that pregnancies that need to be induced are generally problematic in the first place.

Contractions kicked in almost immediately, but they were irregular and mild. Six hours later another pessary was administered and this time the contractions came on astonishingly strong. Four hours later, the pain, I knew, was more than I could bear, and I asked for a shot of diamorphine. But by about 10 P.M. I was only 3 cm dilated, still it was enough for them to break my waters in an attempt to coerce my body into doing what it was meant to be doing. No dice. The contractions continued, but the dilation was unbelievably slow. I realized I could no longer bear the pain unassisted, and I requested an epidural. Sorry, howled for one.

After four attempts to insert the needle into my spine, a consultant anaesthetist was sent for, who managed to get me to sit still long enough to get the needle in. The chief midwife was encouraging, reassuring me I would be able to get this baby out; the doctors supported her.

By morning I was still only 7 cm dilated, so it was agreed I should go on an oxytocin drip to speed up the contractions. The dose was doubled, and then doubled again, as I stalled at 9 cm.

At this point, 30 hours after I had been admitted, the junior registrar raised the C-word. With the natural childbirth lobby ringing in my ears, I asked if I could speak alone to the chief midwife. She agreed with the doctor. Then the senior registrar appeared. Calmly, he laid out the situation. He made no attempt to coerce me into a caesarean and left the decision in my hands.

When I opted to double the oxytocin dose again in a last ditch attempt to get to 10 cm, he went along with me, until the baby's heart rate took a turn for the worse and we caved in to the operating theatre. Once they opened me up it became clear what had happened: my son's head was wedged at an odd angle into my pelvis, meaning he had been unable to descend. To get him out, he had to be pushed back up, before he could be fished out of my abdomen.

Not a pleasant experience, I'll grant you, but the fact remains that without a caesarean, both my son and I would be dead. In the last 50 years, the emancipation of women has been aided by scientific breakthroughs that have allowed us to manage our bodies and our dual roles in society as mothers and individuals. The caesarean section is one such breakthrough, and it should be celebrated as such.

| "The rate of uterine rupture was 50 times higher among women attempting [VBAC] than among women attempting a second vaginal delivery."

Vaginal Birth After Cesarean Birth (VBAC) Is Not Safe for All Women

Melissa M. Kaczmarczyk, Par Sparen, Paul Terry, Sven Cnattingius

Melissa Kaczmarczyk and Paul Terry are researchers at Emory University, and Par Sparen and Sven Cnattingius are researchers at the Karolinska Institutet. In the following viewpoint, they present the findings of their recent study in which they conclude that women who delivered their first child by cesarean section are at higher risk of suffering uterine rupture during an attempt at vaginal birth (VBAC) than women who had given birth vaginally the first time. In addition, the researchers note that the potential for uterine rupture during VBAC is independent of, but can be influenced by, other factors.

Melissa M. Kaczmarczyk, Par Sparen, Paul Terry, Sven Cnattingius, "Risk Factors for Uterine Rupture and Neonatal Consequences of Uterine Rupture: A Population-based Study of Successive Pregnancies in Sweden," *BJOG: An International Journal of Obstetrics and Gynaecology*, vol. 114, October 2007, pp. 1208–1213. Copyright © The Authors. Journal compilation © RCDG 2007. Reproduced by permission of Blackwell Publishers.

As you read, consider the following questions:

1. As reported by the authors, what is the percentage of uterine ruptures among women who attempt VBAC?

2. How much of an increase in risk of uterine rupture did labor induction have during VBAC, according to Kaczmarczyk, Terry, Sparen, and Cnattingius?

3. In addition to prior cesarean sections, what other procedures do the authors list that can cause a uterine scar?

Uterine rupture is a catastrophic event, most often resulting from the tearing of a previous caesarean scar during labour. In addition to previous caesarean, known or suspected risk factors for uterine rupture include induction of labour, maternal age, height, body mass index (BMI), education, cigarette smoking, birthweight, gestational age, instrumental vaginal delivery, and interpregnancy interval. However, effect sizes of these risk factors remain unclear due to methodological differences between studies, such as small sample sizes, lack of population-based studies, varying inclusion criteria, the potential recall bias in case-control studies, and discrepancies in the definition of uterine rupture. In addition, relatively few studies have examined the risk factors for uterine rupture in all women, regardless of history of caesarean.

Although the incidence of uterine rupture is low, with an average incidence of approximately 1% among women attempting vaginal birth after caesarean delivery, the increased maternal and neonatal morbidity and mortality associated with this condition serve to highlight the importance of prevention. Moreover, the rate of caesarean sections, most notably those that are elective, is increasing in developed countries. Consequently, it is possible that rates of uterine rupture will increase in these populations as well.

To further elucidate the risk factors for uterine rupture, we examined data from a nationwide prospective cohort study in Sweden of women attempting vaginal birth in their second delivery. We further assessed the risks of neonatal mortality among women who experienced uterine rupture. . . .

Study Population and Results

In all, there were 327,700 women who delivered first births beginning in 1983 and second consecutive live single births from 1992 through 2001. We excluded 18,101 women who had a caesarean second delivery performed before onset of labour. Women for whom onset of labour in the second delivery could not be determined ($n = 9399$) were also excluded. Thus, the study population included 300,200 women with live single births in second pregnancy. The study was approved by the Research Ethics Committee of Karolinska Institutet. . . .

In our study, among the population of 300,200 women who attempted vaginal birth in the second delivery, 288,038 (95.9%) delivered vaginally and 12,162 (4.1%) by caesarean section. Of the 24,876 women who attempted vaginal birth after a caesarean delivery, 24.7% had an emergency caesarean in the second delivery, while the corresponding ratio among women who were vaginally delivered at first birth was 2.2%. Thus, compared with women who delivered vaginally in the first birth, women who delivered by caesarean section in the first birth were more likely to undergo an unplanned caesarean delivery during their second delivery.

Uterine Rupture

The overall rate of uterine rupture among women with an attempted vaginal birth in their second delivery was 0.91/1000. . . . The rate of uterine rupture among women who attempted vaginal birth after a caesarean section in their first delivery was 9.00/1000 compared with a uterine rupture rate of 0.18/1000 among women without a history of caesarean delivery. Thus, compared with women who had delivered vaginally in the first birth, women who had a caesarean had a substantially increased risk of uterine rupture in their second delivery. Compared with women who experienced a spontaneous onset of delivery, women whose second delivery was induced faced a doubled increase in risk of uterine rupture. Induction of labour was associated with a doubled risk of uterine rupture both among women with a previous caesarean and among women who did not have previous caesarean.

The rate of uterine rupture was substantially higher among women with a vaginal instrumental delivery than among women who did not have a vaginal instrumental delivery (3.46 and 0.83/1000, respectively). However, a vaginal instrumental delivery was not associated with an increased risk in the adjusted analyses. Of all 33 uterine ruptures after a vaginal instrumental delivery, a history of a previous caesarean was present in 29 pregnancies. Thus, the association between vaginal instrumental delivery and risk of uterine rupture was confounded by previous caesarean delivery.

Compared with women whose infants' birthweights ranged from 2499 to 3999 g, women with higher birthweight infants were at increased risk of uterine rupture. The risk of uterine rupture was also increased in women with postterm ($\geq$42 weeks) compared with term (37–41 weeks) pregnancies. A high maternal age ($\geq$35 years) at second delivery and a short maternal stature (height $\leq$164 cm) was also associated with increased risks of uterine rupture in the second delivery. . . .

Neonatal Mortality and Morbidity

Next, we examined uterine rupture in the second delivery and the risk of neonatal mortality. Among 274 women with uterine rupture, there were 14 neonatal deaths (rate 51.09/1000), while the corresponding neonatal death rate among women without uterine rupture was 1.4/1000. Thus, uterine rupture in the second delivery was substantially associated with an increased risk of neonatal mortality.

Apgar score[1] was examined as an indicator of infant morbidity. Uterine rupture in the second delivery was associated with a low (0–6) Apgar score at 5 minutes in the second delivery. In the subgroup of infants who survived the neonatal period, the association between uterine rupture and a low Apgar score was of a similar magnitude.

Induction Agents

In our nationwide Swedish study of more than 300,000 women who underwent labour in their second consecutive single pregnancy, caesarean section in the first delivery was the strongest predictor of uterine rupture. We found that the rate of uterine rupture was 50 times higher among women attempting vaginal birth after a previous caesarean section (rate 9.00/1000) than among women attempting a second vaginal delivery (rate 0.18/1000). This relative risk estimate was attenuated to a 40-fold increase in risk after multivariate adjustments. Thus, this finding is consistent with the relative risk of 40 reported in a large population-based study from Switzerland but is considerably higher than those of three other studies that reported relative risk estimates ranging from 9.0 to 19.5. The adjusted PAR [population attributable risk] of 76.7% in our study was comparable with those from the two studies that also reported the PAR of uterine rupture due to previous caesarean. The increased risk of uterine rupture among women with a history of caesarean delivery may be explained, in part, by induction of labour.

It has been hypothesized that induction agents, such as prostaglandins and oxytocin, that are used to 'ripen' the cervix and to increase uterine contractions can lead to hyperstimulation of the uterus, which may weaken scars from previous caesarean sections and subsequently increase the chances of the scar opening during labour. In a study designed to test

1. Newborn babies are given an Apgar test one minute after birth and five minutes after birth. The score is determined by examining babies for activity, pulse, grimace, appearance, and respiration.

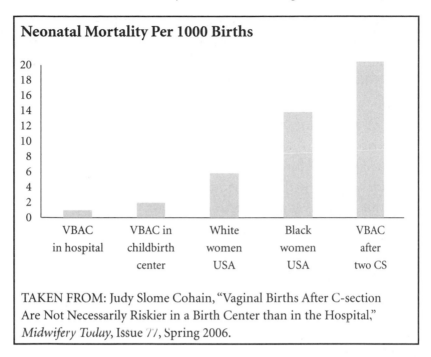

Neonatal Mortality Per 1000 Births

TAKEN FROM: Judy Slome Cohain, "Vaginal Births After C-section Are Not Necessarily Riskier in a Birth Center than in the Hospital," *Midwifery Today*, Issue 77, Spring 2006.

this hypothesis, it was found that women who were induced with prostaglandins ruptured at the site of the uterine scar more often than those who were induced with oxytocin. This is consistent with results from two studies, reporting that prostaglandins are associated with a higher risk of uterine rupture than other induction agents. Reports in the literature concerning the risk of uterine rupture after induction of labour in women with a history of caesarean section attempting vaginal birth are inconsistent. However, comparison of reports concerning the association between uterine rupture and induction are difficult due to the inclusion of low numbers of uterine rupture, differences in the method of induction, dosage of induction agent used, and inclusion criteria.

After adjusting for confounding, we found that induction of labour doubled the risk of uterine rupture compared with spontaneous labour among all women attempting a vaginal second labour. A similarly designed population-based study that examined the relationship of uterine rupture and induction did not find an association between induction and uterine rupture, although the statistical power in that study was limited by the inclusion of only 42 cases of uterine rupture. Although previous caesarean section is the most common cause of a uterine scar, other procedures, such as perforation, uteroplasty, or cornal resection of a uterine injury may result in scarring. Therefore, induction of labour is not only a concern for women with a previous caesarean. This is consistent with our finding that induction was associated with an increased risk of uterine rupture among women with and without a history of caesarean delivery. Also, in rare cases, oxytocin has been found to be associated with rupture of an unscarred uterus, offering further explanation to our finding.

Other Factors

The rate of uterine rupture among women with a history of previous caesarean section whose labour is induced may increase with advancing gestational age. The thickness of lower uterine scars has been shown to decrease as the pregnancy progresses, offering a possible explanation of this increase. A study designed to examine the relationship between gestational age and uterine rupture in women with a history of caesarean delivery found a significant increase in the rate of uterine rupture as gestational age increased in all women undergoing vaginal birth and specifically among women whose labours were induced. In our study, we found a gestational age of ≥42 weeks to be associated with an increased risk of uterine rupture, regardless of caesarean history or onset of labour compared with a gestational age of 37–41 weeks. This is consistent with the findings of a case-control study, which included 134 cases of uterine rupture but contradicts the findings of three other studies. This contradiction may be due to inclusion of a low number of uterine ruptures.

Instrumental vaginal delivery, including ventouse (vacuum extraction) and forceps delivery, has been previously identified as a risk factor for maternal and fetal complications. The risk of uterine rupture associated with instrumental vaginal delivery is unclear due to an absence of previous studies. We found that the rate of uterine rupture was higher among women who underwent an instrumental vaginal delivery than among women who did not, although this difference was not significant after controlling for confounding by previous caesarean section. Instrumental vaginal delivery is often performed in women with a history of caesarean delivery to minimize the risk of the uterine scar opening during labour. In a case-control study of women with one previous caesarean section who attempted vaginal birth in subsequent delivery, uterine rupture was found to be significantly associated with instrumental vaginal delivery. This further emphasises the need for the prudent management of labour in women with a history of caesarean delivery.

Birthweight of more than 4500 g has also been associated with an increase in maternal and fetal morbidity and mortality. Consistent with a population-based cohort study of women with one previous caesarean delivery attempting a vaginal birth, we found a nearly doubled increase in the risk of uterine rupture among high birthweight infants ($\geq$4000 g) compared with infants weighing less than 4000 g at birth. This finding contradicts several other reports in which high birthweight was not associated with an increase in uterine rupture. In light of a recent trend of increasing birthweight in Western countries, it is imperative that the association between high birthweight and uterine rupture be further explored.

In addition to the aforementioned risk factors, we also found high maternal age ($\geq$35 years) to nearly double the risk of uterine rupture compared with women 25–29 years. This is consistent with a report of a 3.2-fold increased risk of uterine rupture among women with a history of previous caesarean

≥30 years compared with women <30 years. As the birthrate for women older than 30 years continues to rise, more women are at risk for uterine rupture, especially when attempting a trial of labour after a previous caesarean delivery.

As the rates of caesarean section and induction of labour continue to rise in developed countries, the number of women at risk for uterine rupture is also increasing. Although the rates of uterine rupture are low in the developed world, there are serious consequences associated with uterine rupture. For example, among 274 cases of uterine rupture in our study, there were 14 (5%) cases of neonatal death, a more than 60-fold increase in the risk of neonatal mortality after the occurrence of a uterine rupture, compared with deliveries in which a rupture did not occur. This finding is comparable with several studies that reported prenatal or neonatal mortality rates of 5–6% in deliveries in which a uterine rupture occurred, and even higher rates have been reported. We also found an increased risk of low Apgar score for infants delivered after a uterine rupture compared with infants delivered without the occurrence of such an event, a finding that was also consistent with those of other studies. . . .

In conclusion, our large, population-based prospective cohort study has confirmed the reports of previous studies. We not only confirmed a strong association between a previous caesarean delivery and risk of uterine rupture in subsequent pregnancy but also that other factors including high maternal age, induction of labour, and high birthweight increased the risk of uterine rupture. All these factors are becoming increasingly prevalent in the pregnant population, which highlights the importance of active management of labour aiming to detect early signs of and preventing threatening uterine rupture during labour.

Periodical Bibliography

The following articles have been selected to supplement the diverse views presented in this chapter.

Cheryl Anderson and Teena M. McGuiness	"Do Teenage Mothers Experience Childbirth as Traumatic?" *Journal of Psychosocial Nursing & Mental Health Services*, vol. 46, no. 4, April 2008.
Lynn Clark Callister	"Cesarean Birth Rates: Global Trends," *MCN: The American Journal of Maternal Child Nursing*, vol. 33, no. 2, March/April 2008.
Stacey Escoffery and Susan Dickman	"VBAC Victory!" *Mothering*, September/October 2006.
Liam Fitzpatrick	"The LaborMarket," *Time International*, March 31, 2008.
Jenny Hope	"Women 'Should Be Warned over the Pain of Childbirth,'" *Daily Mail*, March 14, 2008.
Alfredo F. Gei and Luis D. Pacheco	"Forceps: Still an Option?" *Current Women's Health Reviews*, vol. 4, no. 1, 2008.
Deborah Kotz	"A Risky Rise in C-Sections," *U.S. News and World Report*, April 7, 2008.
Clarissa Kripke	"Repeat Cesarean Delivery vs. Planned Induction of Labor," *American Family Physician*, vol. 76, no. 7, October 1, 2007.
Penny Simkin	"What Makes a Good Birth and Why Does it Matter?" *International Journal of Childbirth Education*, September 2006.
Jennie Yabroff	"Birth, the American Way," *Newsweek*, January 28, 2008.
Gulay Yildirim and Nezihe Kizilkaya Beji	"Effects of Pushing Techniques in Birth on Mother and Fetus: Randomized Study," *Birth*, vol. 35, no. 1, March 2008.

CHAPTER 2

What Are the Best Conditions for Childbirth?

Chapter Preface

Until recently, women had only two options for where to give birth: home or hospital. In the 1960s, women began searching for a place in between. They wanted all of the comforts of home with some of the safety of the hospital setting. The birth center was created to fill this gap. Birth centers are operated by midwives and other birthing professionals, such as doulas, and focus on mother-friendly birth practices. In an effort to not lose patients to freestanding birth centers, many hospitals have added in-house birth centers to their usual options for birthing patients. Given that more women are choosing to have their babies in birth centers than ever before, it is important to consider their advantages and disadvantages.

Birth centers are typically geared more toward laboring women's desires than are hospitals. They give women more control over their labor and delivery and provide a less clinical setting than the typical hospital maternity ward. Birth centers generally provide personalized services, allow eating and drinking during labor, offer nonmedical pain management tools, and do not restrict mobility during labor. According to the Baby Center Advisory Board, "Birth centers offer a low-tech, high-touch, personalized, and comfortable place for childbirth." In addition, a 2005 study published in the *British Medical Journal* revealed that the infant mortality rate was roughly the same for midwife-attended births as for hospital births, but that the rate of cesarean sections for out-of-hospital births was 26 percent lower than hospital births. Many people consider birth centers an ideal option for women who would like more supervision than a home birth and less intervention than a hospital birth.

Despite the benefits, birth centers are not for all women. Most health care providers, including birth center professionals, discourage women with high-risk pregnancies from using a birth center. Although centers are equipped with IVs, oxygen, and other low-tech emergency interventions, women undergoing problematic deliveries must be transferred to a hospital if they need cesarean sections and anesthesia. In addition, the postpartum stay at birth centers is much shorter than at hospitals, which gives health professionals less time to discover potential after-birth complications in mother or baby. The U.S. Department of Health and Human Services recommends that women who are diabetic, who are expecting multiples, or who have preeclampsia give birth at a hospital rather than a birth center.

As more choices become available to pregnant women, health care professionals will continue to rise to the challenge. The American Pregnancy Association reminds women that "birthing centers can vary significantly, so you will want to investigate carefully their philosophy of care; review mission statements, objectives, and interview personnel to find the one that fits your birth plan." As demonstrated by the authors in the following chapter, all parties involved share a similar goal—to ensure the safest and most comfortable birth possible—but opinions vary widely as to the best way to achieve that goal.

> "Birth is a personal choice that women
> need not surrender to others."

Women Should Be
Given Choices About
Where to Give Birth

Cynthia Overgard

In the following viewpoint, Cynthia Overgard, a certified Hyp-noBirthing practitioner and writer, argues that women should be given the choice to give birth in an environment that best suits their needs. By discussing her own pregnancy and childbirth experiences, she asserts that women should educate themselves about the three main places to give birth: hospitals, home, and birth centers. Disappointed by her doctor's attitudes about fetal monitoring and cesarean sections, she discovers a birth center that offers her more options.

As you read, consider the following questions:

1. What does Overgard cite as the national cesarean rate?
2. What effect can doulas have on labor and delivery, according to Overgard?

Cynthia Overgard, "Off Her Back: Wary of Her Obstetrician's High C-section Rate, She Left the Practice and Found Her Way to a Beautiful Natural Birth," *Mothering*, vol. 145, November–December, 2007, pp. 58–64. Reproduced by permission of the author.

3. As the author explains, how many sonograms are recommended during a low-risk pregnancy?

I was pregnant; the notion of making a commitment to natural delivery in a birth center—without doctors or pain relief of any kind on the premises—was furthest from my mind. Like many other newly pregnant women, I reluctantly envisioned my hospital birth to mirror that of every other actual and fictitious birth I had ever heard about: Agonized and disoriented, I would be rushed urgently into a medical scene amid bright lights, confusing equipment, and an assortment of intense, unfamiliar faces. I envisioned myself in the usual, dreaded position of lying on my back, my knees bent, nobly trying to resist an epidural for as long as possible before acquiescing to that temptation, praying all the while that my baby and I would not be harmed by the anesthesia. This vision, unsettling as it was, had been far too deeply ingrained by society and mainstream media for me to have realized that I actually had a choice in the matter. . . .

One evening, while conducting research on the Internet about pregnancy and childbirth, I happened on a Web site in which a mother shared the details of her natural homebirth. Within moments, a longing formed within me—that easy, natural birth was indeed possible; I just didn't believe it was possible for me. Emotionally, unready to consider it further, I gave myself precisely what I needed in that moment: permission to stay on course with a conventional hospital birth, like every other rational, educated, metropolitan New York woman I knew. . . .

I began to educate myself about the complexity of our nation's obstetrics industry. My education came at a cost: an ever-increasing fear of the very hospital birth I had planned. Stunned to learn that doctors were held to revenue targets at the hospitals in which they practiced, a cynicism grew within me. Soon I understood the risks associated with medical intervention in the delivery room: Even seemingly, innocuous procedures, such as the use of an electronic fetal monitor, suddenly looked like threats. I discovered that each form of intervention would increase the odds, often dramatically, that further, more drastic procedure would then be necessary. Electronic fetal monitors, Pitocin, cesarean sections, anatomies, epidurals, episiotomies—they all formed an entanglement of interdependent risks and complications.

An Unsettling Appointment

At my 12-week checkup, I asked my own obstetrician a straightforward question: her cesarean rate. Her response was that she had no idea; the obstetrics practice hadn't bothered to calculate those numbers in years.

"The national average is around 27 percent [2003]," I said. "Would you guess this practice comes in higher or lower?"

"Definitely higher," she said.

Anxiously, I demanded to know how much higher. "Is it greater than thirty percent? Thirty-five percent?" She looked at me regretfully. I pressed on. "Forty percent?!"

She finally nodded. "Yes, at least, but I don't have exact numbers."

Incredulously, I asked why they were performing such an extraordinarily high rate of C-sections. Were they elective, or did the obstetricians in her practice really feel that life-or-death situations were so frequently at hand?

"Yes, some are elective," she began. "Many women feel they would prefer to have their own doctor perform a cesarean rather than take the chance of delivering vaginally with a less familiar doctor from the same practice."

And you actually give merit to that choice? I wanted to ask. Major surgery, unnecessarily performed as a matter of familiarity and convenience?. . .

That early in my pregnancy, I still wasn't aware of the medical risks associated with cesareans for both mother and baby, nor was I aware of the respiratory benefits a baby re-

ceives from its passage through the birth canal. I was also un-
prepared for the "litigation argument" so frequently used by
obstetricians, which, though arguably legitimate, successfully
manipulates pregnant couples into inferring that a cesarean is
actually the safer method of childbirth.

I nodded soberly as she spoke, reminding myself that I
was strong and adaptable, and that the only outcome that
truly mattered was a healthy baby.

In the following days, as I became increasingly uncomfortable with my obstetrician's aggressive approach to C-sections,
I learned that hiring a doula—a labor assistant—would reduce my odds of experiencing medical complications during
the birth. My husband, Eric, and I decided that we had nothing to lose. When we hired our doula, we unknowingly took
our first step away from conventional labor preparation, and
we began our eventual transition to childbirth independence.

Choosing a Birth Center

At the completion of my 16-week checkup, my obstetrician
caught me off guard when she requested I come back for a
visit between our regularly scheduled visits. Rather than re-
turn at 20 weeks, she suggested I squeeze in an extra checkup
at 18 weeks so she could perform another "routine" sono-
gram. With four fetal ultrasounds already under my belt, I
was both confused by and uncomfortable with her request. I
had recently learned of the controversy surrounding fetal ultrasounds, and understood that three sonograms during an
entire pregnancy was the standard recommendation. . . .

The following morning I telephoned my obstetrician's office and asked them to prepare a copy of my medical file: I
was leaving the practice. And, just like that, I allowed room
for an alternative birth choice to present itself.

Later that night, I wound up in a disheartening, circular
thought process: Where would we deliver our baby? Then my
husband and I discovered that Connecticut's only freestanding

What About Hypnosis for Childbirth?

Hypnosis is used in medical and dental [procedures] with great success by patients who have life-threatening allergies to anesthetics, allowing them to undergo surgeries with no drugs and no pain. We know therefore that the mind can be trained to experience discomfort as only pressure, and that is what is achieved in childbirth hypnosis as well. In addition, with labor, the more relaxation the mother experiences, the more comfort she will have, and the depth of relaxation necessary can easily be achieved with hypnosis, as physical relaxation is learned and practiced daily in preparation for birth using guided visualizations followed by positive hypnotic suggestions. When the critical conscious mind is by-passed with hypnosis, the inner mind can literally be reprogrammed to believe that birth will be comfortable, easy, and joyous. Software for your mind!

Kerry Tuschoff,
"HypnoBirth: What Is It and How Does It Work?" 2008,
www.childbirthsolutions.com.

birth center was an hour's drive away from us. We decided to visit the Connecticut Childbirth and Women's Center the following day to take a tour of the facility.

After an enjoyable, hour-long question-and-answer session with the midwife director, we were led away from the examination rooms and upstairs to the beautiful birthing suites. I was struck by the setting—the plush double bed, hardwood floors, and floral window dressings were reminiscent of a New England bed-and-breakfast. We walked through the bedroom and into the large, marble bathroom, complete with a freestanding shower for two and Jacuzzi bathtub. As we walked, the midwife said, "You can deliver on the bed, in the birthing chair, on the floor, standing up, sitting down, lying on your side, in the shower, or in the tub. We ask only that you not deliver lying on your back—it would be uncomfortable for you, and it's least optimal for the baby."

"Is it ever difficult for you to receive the baby if the mother chooses an unconventional position?"

"No," she smiled. "Remember, this isn't about our convenience and comfort; it's about yours."

From that point on, I kept every remaining prenatal appointment at the birth center, cheerfully driving an hour each way through the cold winter. . . .

A Simple Labor and Delivery

When I went into labor, my contractions were immediately three to four minutes apart, and I was six centimeters dilated when we arrived at the birth center an hour later. The midwives were cheerful on our pre-dawn arrival. One exclaimed, "Just imagine, Cynthia, you're going to meet your baby today!"

In the warm Jacuzzi bathtub, with my husband and four confident, smiling women encircling me, I envisioned my body opening up. I reminded myself that the more I relaxed, the faster I would dilate. The HypnoBirthing technique apparently worked—I was at ten centimeters within the hour. I had been taking long sips of water and engaging in relaxed conversation between contractions. The pushing stage, however, was more intense, and required all my focus and energy. Our doula held a cool washcloth to my forehead while pouring warm water over my shoulders. She whispered, "Look outside, Cynthia. The sun is rising."

Her comment awakened me from the intensity of the moment. The March morning was clear; reds and oranges spread abundantly across the mountain range. I was happy for our baby: what a beautiful day to be born. More important, our baby would be born to a mother who felt calm, safe, and loved. I was overcome with gratitude for whatever serendipitous course of events had brought us here, and for the relief I felt when I suddenly thought, If I weren't delivering here, at this very moment, then where?

From beginning to end, my labor had lasted just three-and-a-half hours—extremely short for a first-time laborer, but precisely the average for mothers who practice HypnoBirthing, I was told. Despite the fast labor, my small frame, and my baby's hefty size of 8 pounds, 14 ounces, I had one tear so minor that it required only a single stitch.

When the post-birth examination was complete, we were encouraged to take a few hours of private family time to rest in bed. Nestled snugly between mother and father, our son, Alexander, gazed contentedly into our eyes.

Birth is a personal choice that women need not surrender to others. Making that choice takes—and breeds—emotional courage. My husband and I had conducted countless hours of research, challenged one another with complicated questions ranging from the logistical to the moral, and consistently faced opposition from a well-meaning society. Eventually, we quieted the outside noise and discovered our own articulate voices. We discovered a great empowerment, both individually and as a couple. And of all that we learned, one truth spoke most clearly: It is the right of every woman to pursue her own child's birth—at home, hospital, or birth center—with the information, honor, and freedom to which she is entitled.

> *"Pushing 'choice' in selecting home as opposed to hospital birth is still unhelpful to many."*

Focusing on Choices About Where to Give Birth Detracts from the Purpose of Childbirth

Margaret McCartney

In the following viewpoint, Margaret McCartney, a general practitioner from Glasgow, Scotland, expresses her concern about the way in which birth is depicted in modern culture. She argues that making women believe that childbirth should be a magical experience, and that they can control the outcomes of that experience by choosing the best place to give birth, takes away from the point of a successful and safe labor and delivery: a healthy baby. McCartney asserts that an overemphasis on choice leads some new mothers to feel like failures if they did not have the "perfect" birth.

As you read, consider the following questions:

1. According to a Cochrane Library review, what do home-like birth settings offer?

2. What difference does McCartney give between the death rates of mothers and babies in a home-type setting versus a hospital setting?

3. According to the author, what is one of the greatest medical advances in history?

A hundred years ago, pregnancy was tough and labour was brutal. You would aspire to having lots of children, mainly because a few were expected to die either during birth or in early childhood.

The mortality rate for pregnancy and childbirth in the [United Kingdom] UK today is tiny in comparison. Our concerns are usually altogether different. Months before becoming pregnant, many women stock up on folic acid—vitamins taken during pregnancy that reduce the risk of spina bifida. The timing of pregnancy is often carefully planned and conception is confirmed within days using ultra-sensitive pregnancy tests. And then there's the all-important question of the birth.

Health secretary Patricia Hewitt, in a slightly swashbuckling role, announced this week [May 20, 2006] that she was to "challenge the assumption" that hospital births were safer than home deliveries. The Department of Health says: "We are committed to offering all women the choice of how and where they give birth."

There is no doubt that the home [versus] hospital debate is a messy one, laced with emotionally fraught anecdotes of either natural childbirth success or home birth tragedy.

Home Versus Hospital Birth

There are two papers worth noting on this subject. One is a systematic review, published by the Cochrane Library [an independent organization that reviews medical literature for the

Consequences of the Midwife Shortage

As many as 1,000 unborn babies die each year because doctors and midwives are overstretched or too poorly trained to spot danger signs, an expert claims.

A quarter of the 4,000 stillbirths which take place in the UK annually could be avoided if medical staff took action during pregnancy, says Professor Jason Gardosi, director of the Perinatal Institute in Birmingham.

Britain has one of the worst records for stillbirths in western Europe, with double the rate in Italy, Sweden and Switzerland.

Source: Daniel Martin,
"1,000 Babies Die 'Unnecessarily' Each Year
Due to Midwife Shortage," Daily Mail, September 24, 2007.

public]. This high quality assembly of all the current evidence states: "Home-like birth settings are intended for women who prefer to avoid medical intervention during labor and birth but who either do not wish or cannot have a home birth . . . trials suggest modest benefits, including decreased medical intervention and higher rates of spontaneous vaginal birth, breastfeeding, and maternal satisfaction. However, there may be an added risk of perinatal mortality." (Home-like birth often refers to a low-tech unit, meant to be somewhere between a home and labor ward but sited in a hospital and staffed by midwives.)

The second paper, published in the *British Medical Journal*, examined the outcomes of more than 5,000 planned home-births in Canada. It concludes: "Planned home birth for low risk women in North America using certified professional midwives was associated with lower rates of medical intervention but similar intrapartum and neonatal mortality to that of low risk hospital births in the United States."

In other words, there does not seem to be a huge difference between death rates of either baby or mother in delivering at home-type settings compared with hospital, and there do seem to be advantages of less medical intervention. However pushing "choice" in selecting home as opposed to hospital birth is still unhelpful to many.

Firstly, there seems to be an aching double standard. While labor is being "demedicalised", pregnancy itself is a veritable feast of medical intervention. We can now test for things that our grandmothers could not have imagined. Blood and ultrasound tests are used to gauge the odds of having certain conditions such as Down syndrome, spina bifida or kidney abnormalities that may lead to infections when the child is born.

These are optional but many accept them meekly as being "for the best". There is even more testing outside the NHS [National Health Service, England's publicly funded health care system]—for "reassurance" as people are inclined to say. A few hundred pounds will buy an ultrasound scan to measure skin folds at the foetal neck. This nuchal fold scanning, to predict Down syndrome, is usually only offered on the NHS to those at high risk.

Secondly, when it comes to home births, there are, unfortunately, a huge number of women whose feelings go unstudied. Many women will have satisfying home birth experiences but, in every sphere of my life, I know others who feel as though they "failed" in some way. Some were advised that a homebirth was too risky while others were scooped up, mid-labor, by an ambulance and went on to have an emergency section in hospital. This may be based on anecdote but no one seems to be assessing this clearly adverse effect in a scientific way.

This is an enormous paradox. During pregnancy, we often accept anything offered, no matter how potentially intrusive the test or how difficult it is to know what to do with the result. But by opting for more home births, we are going down a low-tech route that is more "natural", less "invasive".

Healthy Child Is a By-Product

Meantime, the healthy child has become a by-product of the modern maternal experience rather than the purpose of it. We have been sold the myth that the outcome of birth should include some kind of esoteric "satisfaction"; that maternal fulfillment lies in having some kind of spiritual birth experience. A lot of women never get this feeling, no matter what their births are like. At such a delicate and tender time, this invites a sense of failure.

Even the issue of pain relief in labor is politicized. This is surely one of the greatest medical advances yet is viewed by some childbirth and pregnancy organizations as a "last resort". As a result, many women who end up requesting it feel guilty or second rate. There may be disadvantages in using some forms of pain relief in labor but it is hardly the evil it is sometimes suggested to be.

There is also the problem that midwives are in short supply and the additional numbers needed to staff home births are unlikely to be available any time soon. Hospital labor wards, which deal with higher risk deliveries, are permanently short staffed.

Do we really want childbirth to masquerade as competitive maternal nirvana with prizes for least pain relief? Or indeed, is pregnancy to be a tense obstacle course? The distorted focus on "the experience" of birth means that the first few weeks of having a new baby are often a let-down. "Failing" to be admitted to the cult of perfect childbirth only fuels the emotional and exhausting few weeks afterwards. We would be better instead using our energy to consider carefully which antenatal tests we choose and to view birth as an objective— the production of a healthy mother and baby.

> "Giving birth at home can be just as safe and can even lead to more positive outcomes for both mother and child."

Home Births Are Safe

Janelle Weiner

In the following viewpoint, Janelle Weiner, high school teacher and mother of two children, argues that home birth can be just as safe as giving birth in a hospital. She explains that women are influenced by the images of childbirth in the media and have a difficult time thinking that labor and delivery can be calm and free of external stresses. Although she acknowledges the usefulness of hospital intervention in case of life-threatening emergencies, her own experiences and research have convinced her that a family-centered approach to childbirth is the best option.

As you read, consider the following questions:

1. How does the author define shoulder dystocia?
2. How much more likely are women to die because of complications associated with cesarean sections than with vaginal births, according to Janelle Weiner?
3. How does Weiner explain Pitocin?

Women in the US make a lot of choices before their babies are born, from which foods to eat, to which birth preparation class to take, to how to decorate the nursery. For most, however, there's no question where their babies will be born: a "bun in the oven" means feet in the stirrups for a delivery in the hospital—accepted as the safe, modern location for giving birth.

But studies show that giving birth at home can be just as safe and can even lead to more positive outcomes for both mother and child. . . .

The idea that birth can be a normal experience flies in the face of all the cultural information disseminated on the subject by reality and fictional TV shows alike. Birth is a subject that naturally fits into the dramatic arc that viewers expect, and it is exploited and dramatized for entertainment purposes regularly. We see women swearing, screaming and panicking as they bring their babies into the world. Any woman who has been pregnant also knows that friends and family seem compelled to share their own birth horror stories as her belly grows.

Unfortunately, this view of birth is the only one many women in the United States are exposed to before experiencing it themselves, and the message is clear: birth is dangerous and only the obstetrician can save you. Hospitals are necessary, to be sure, and they are valuable in complicated births, but there is evidence that women who are at low risk for complications—and the majority are—can safely give birth at home. . . .

Hospital Birth Interventions

The issue of choice is often cited as a reason for having an out-of-hospital birth. In the hospital, the obstetrician and a group of nurses usually manage a woman's labor. How it proceeds depends on the protocol of each particular hospital. In this context, the laboring mother often becomes a passive par-

Studies Indicate That Homebirths Are Safe

Safety in childbirth is measured by how many mothers and babies die and how many survive childbirth in less than perfect health.

Studies done comparing hospital and out-of-hospital births indicate fewer deaths, injuries and infections for homebirths supervised by a trained attendant than for hospital births. No such studies indicate that hospitals have better outcomes than homebirths.

Jane Tipton,
"Is Homebirth For You? 6 Myths About Childbirth Exposed," 1990,
www.gentlebirth.com.

ticipant in one of the most important experiences of her life. In contrast, the birth process unfolds more naturally and without intervention when a woman gives birth at home with a midwife—and this is without risk to the baby, according to a large-scale study of 5,418 women in the United States and Canada that was published by the *British Medical Journal* in 2005.

"Planned homebirth for low-risk women in North America using certified professional midwives was associated with lower rates of medical intervention," according to the study, "but similar intrapartum and neonatal mortality to that of low-risk hospital births in the United States."

The women in the study who gave birth at home received episiotomies—this is an incision to the perineum, the area of skin between the vagina and anus—2.1% of the time, compared to 33% of those who labored in the hospital. Only 3.7% of women in the study who planned homebirths eventually had cesarean sections, compared to 19% of those in hospitals.

In short, women were receiving interventions in the traditional hospital setting that were apparently unnecessary.

It's typically believed a hospital takes much of the risk out of having a baby, but the women who give birth there may be taking risks they haven't considered. For example, shoulder dystocia, in which the baby's shoulder becomes stuck in the birth canal after the head has emerged, can be caused by the use of forceps or a vacuum—two tools sometimes used by hospitals. Another fact not generally known is that women are three times more likely to die during or from complications associated with cesarean sections than with vaginal births, according to the American College of Obstetrics and Gynecology.

Licensed Midwife Rachel Fox-Tierney of Birth Stream Midwifery in Davis, California, notes, "There is always the risk of unnecessary intervention. Walking in the door is an intervention in the process of birth. The birth process works best when women are allowed to follow what their bodies need them to do. When there is a foreign environment, when there are unfamiliar people, procedures and protocols that don't take into account how a woman's own individual body works, and a lack of respect for [both] her privacy and faith in a woman's ability to give birth naturally and normally, the birth process has been interfered with and is [therefore] less smooth."

One of the problems with giving birth in modern hospitals in the United States is that rising operational costs have led to an environment that is increasingly concerned with efficiency and protocol at the expense of personalized care. Where the health of a mother and infant is concerned, this confusion of priorities can have serious consequences. For example, hospitals routinely give women a drug called Pitocin while they are in labor in order to speed up contractions which can lead to fetal distress, one of the primary conditions leading to

C-sections. Ironically, the choice to speed up labor often ends up costing hospitals more in the end.

An aversion to the impersonal nature of hospital care is what led Mya Dudzik of Sacramento [California] to give birth to her third, fourth, and fifth children at home. She had nothing against hospitals after giving birth to the first two, but when she found out she was pregnant with her third child, she felt the medical staff treated the pregnancy as a "nonevent." Dudzik decided on a homebirth so "it would be celebrated more," she says. "I'm not the type of person who thinks I'm going to die in the hospital. I do (homebirth) for my own personal reasons. I felt safe both ways. I was seeking it out not because I hate hospitals. It was a more magical experience at home."

A Personal Decision

My own decision to give birth at home was partly personal.

When I became pregnant with my second baby, [my good friend and registered nurse Tuesday] Benavidez suggested I look into homebirth. I hesitated. No, I resisted. I had fretted throughout her pregnancy because of her choice, especially when she went two weeks past her due date, but then she successfully gave birth at home to a 9-pound, 6-ounce baby with shoulder dystocia—a condition that almost certainly would have led to serious intervention in a hospital. I began researching it.

Even after I decided to give birth at home, though, my intellectual side continued to debate my choice. As one might guess, most of the issues began with, "What if . . .?" As I came closer to my estimated due date, though, my anxiety melted away. More and more, I felt the same delicious anticipation that I had felt before my first son's birth, partly because, over a combined 30-plus years of experience, my midwives were no strangers to complications.

With all the emphasis that homebirth moms place on having a positive birth experience, one might wonder if we have lost sight of the most important thing of all—having a healthy baby in our arms. Most women who choose homebirth, however, do so because how labor unfolds or is managed is directly related to the outcome.

Research has shown, for example, that a negative birth experience can lead to postpartum depression. There is also the difficulty in taking care of one's baby if a cesarean is involved, as well as the aforementioned risk of maternal death from this complicated surgery. In addition, some pain medications used in labor can interfere with a newborn's ability to nurse.

The Drama of Hospital Births

In contrast, a positive birth experience can have physical and psychological benefits.

"It is the most powerful experience of your life," Benavidez said, "no matter how you have your baby—C-section, hospital, home—you'll gain from that experience strength that you'll be able to use in all aspects of your life. One can never have too much encouragement in that area. It's maybe the most powerful spiritual experience and can help raise your self-esteem. Women need that in this society."

The numbers show birthing outside of a hospital doesn't have to be the dramatic, tension-filled event frequently portrayed on TV and that many women have experienced in hospital births. A growing number of women are declining the real-life drama of being wheeled into the operating room for an emergency C-section in favor of giving birth in the safety of their own homes.

Groups in the United States, such as Citizens for Midwifery, are working to increase access to information about the safe and family-centered model of care midwives provide.

Fox-Tierney attributes an increased awareness of alternative birth choices to communication between women, partly through the Internet.

"I think that whenever there have been changes in the way [women] have chosen to give birth and who their practitioners are—it is consumer driven," says Fox-Tierney. "With Internet, women can get access to information in ways they never could before. Even if in your neck of the woods there are no midwives, you can hear about Jane Smith in Oregon who had a homebirth. I would hope that women are taking charge of their own health care and recognizing the benefits of midwifery care and their own ability to give birth in less technologically driven ways."

| "Even with high-risk patients (resent-
fully) excluded, homebirth is risky."

Home Births Are Not Safe for Some Women

Catherine Bennett

Catherine Bennett is a columnist for The Observer *and a regular contributor to* The Guardian, *in which the following viewpoint appears. She argues that home births are not safe for all women. Furthermore, she states that Great Britain's government-funded National Health Service should not indulge the whims of women who want to deliver their babies at home, especially when patients with far more serious conditions are being denied help. Given that thousands of impoverished women in the developing world die during childbirth, Bennett asserts that Great Britain's women should take advantage of the safety of hospital care during labor and delivery.*

As you read, consider the following questions:

1. According to the World Health Organization (WHO), how many women die each year in childbirth?

Catherine Bennett, "While Women in the Developing World Are Dying in Childbirth, Why Are We Fetishising Doing It at Home?" *The Guardian*, April 5, 2007. Copyright © 2007 Guardian Newspapers Limited. Reproduced by permission of Guardian News Service, LTD.

2. According to the WHO, what is the difference in rate of women dying in pregnancy and childbirth in developing countries compared to those in developed countries?

3. According to the author, what are some of the services being denied to Great Britain's citizens by the National Health Service?

Even if earthly arrangements were, in every other respect, irreproachable, human parturition would be fatal to the theory of intelligent design. Unless, as someone has recently speculated, God is a psychopath as well as a top designer, who chose to punish women for original sin by tearing up an earlier scheme for pain-free birth. Whatever the reason—divine malice, or the evolutionary conflict between big brains and pelvises tilted for walking upright—the consecquences for at least 529,000 women a year are fatal. The World Health Organization [WHO] has estimated that this may be only half the true number.

As you'd expect, the deaths are unevenly spread. "In some developing regions", the WHO reported recently, "a woman has a one in 16 chance of dying in pregnancy and childbirth. This compares with a one in 2,800 risk for a woman from a developed region". A risk so low as to seem, to many women in those developed regions, completely negligible. Natural childbirth campaigners routinely challenge what they perceive to be the pathologising of childbirth with their mantra, "pregnancy is not a medical condition". Such is the hostility to medicine among some natural-birth enthusiasts that doctors are presented as a greater risk to a mother's health than childbirth.

The organizers of Aims (Association for Improvements in the Maternity Services), for instance, provide for women whose [general practitioners] GPs have identified them as high risk (and thus ineligible for home birth) this template letter to the local director of midwifery services: "I have care-

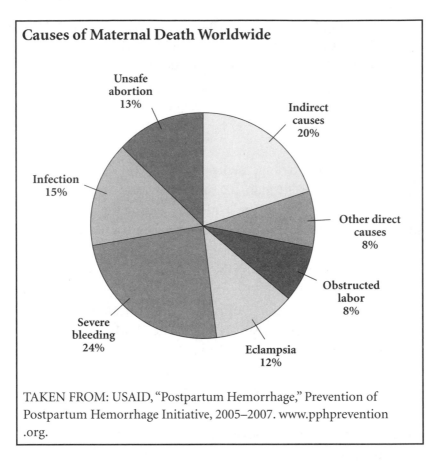

Causes of Maternal Death Worldwide

Unsafe abortion
13%

Indirect causes
20%

Infection
15%

Other direct causes
8%

Obstructed labor
8%

Severe bleeding
24%

Eclampsia
12%

TAKEN FROM: USAID, "Postpartum Hemorrhage," Prevention of Postpartum Hemorrhage Initiative, 2005–2007. www.pphprevention .org.

fully considered the risks of home birth and compared them with the risks of hospital birth and I am not prepared to risk my, or my baby's health, by being delivered in hospital". Other mothers are so opposed to intervention that they aim for "freebirth", or unassisted childbirth. Aims informs them that this very traditional choice (last popular when our ancestors were still crawling) is perfectly legal: "The woman herself cannot be prosecuted for birthing her own baby".

Indulging a Minority Group

If free birth remains a minority interest, the principle that—for western women—satisfactory childbirth involves far more than a safe delivery has long been mainstream. It underpinned the [United Kingdom's] Department of Health's Changing Childbirth in 1993, and was repeated this week, with [Health Secretary] Patricia Hewitt's offer of homebirths for all: "We want it to be as safe and satisfying for every woman in every part of the country as it can be".

An insincere promise, obviously, given that many maternity units are still appallingly understaffed (as well as dirty and ill equipped). And a rash one, perhaps, given that "satisfying" to certain mothers, now means an episode of ecstasy. "Labour can be pleasurable, not painful, and it sometimes builds up to a crescendo at birth," an independent midwife explained recently. The least ambitious alumni of natural childbirth classes are likely to plan, if not an actual crescendo, a combination of a pool, dimmed lights, whale music, and a drug-defying triumph over pain that will transform the humdrum business of childbirth into something heroic and meaningful.

So long as their babies are safe, there is, of course, no reason why Britain's birth fetishists should not attempt, and then advertise on dedicated Web sites, their prodigious feats of home-dilation, and skill in outwitting anxious midwives: "My hubby got the waterproof shower curtains out at this point." There seems no reason, however, why this peculiarly middle-class form of self-absorption should be indulged by the rationing, supposedly rational NHS [National Health Service, England's publicly funded health care system]. Merciless when denying life-prolonging drugs to cancer patients, indifferent to pensioners who are still being humiliated on mixed wards, Hewitt has instead prioritized the demands of that limited group of women who believe that state-funded childbirth should be tailored around their own lifestyle choices, as set out in bossy, novella-length birth plans: "Please keep the room as quiet as possible during the second stage," goes a suggested plan by home-birth advocate Angela Horn. "I would like to minimize distractions at this time. If you need to discuss matters with the second midwife, please could you do so very quietly and preferably out of earshot!" There is little evidence on the Web sites of this kind of demand emanating from pregnant women who live in cramped or uncomfortable conditions, for whom a stay in hospital might even be welcome.

With the end of home visits by GPs, is there another condition to which the NHS will respond by sending out one, or two, sometimes three specialists to spend hours in the patient's home? While terminally sick and elderly patients are dispatched to die among strangers in medic-free wards, Hewitt has accepted that our sturdiest, most articulate primigravidae should be encouraged to summon medical staff to their sitting rooms, for reasons which, when they are not to do with the sacred, or personal self-esteem, seem largely to relate to convenience: "It was perfect, being able to relax and recover at home, instantly, knowing everything was at hand . . ."

Including the emergency services. Even with high-risk patients (resentfully) excluded, home birth is risky. When complications do arise, the outcome "is likely to be less favourable" in hospital (The National Institute for Health and Clinical Excellence regrets the poor quality of evidence on relative safety). And sometimes, even the most fanatical home-birthers have to accept that natural isn't synonymous with safe. "Our own birth story was as far from perfect as we could have envisaged," posts a mother whose home birth was replaced by a caesarean, following a diagnosis of pre-eclampsia. "My overwhelming feelings in the 48 hours after the birth were of failure." The baby, you gather, was completely fine.

> *"Your birth environment and the people caring for you during your labor and delivery can dramatically impact how you will perceive your childbirth experience."*

Hospital Births Can Be Safe

William Camann and Kathryn Alexander

William Camann and Kathryn Alexander are coauthors of Easy Labor: Every Woman's Guide to Choosing Less Pain and More Joy During Childbirth, *from which the following viewpoint is excerpted. They argue that a hospital is not only the most common place where delivery occurs in America, it can also be a safe and caring environment. They note that women choose to give birth in hospitals because they want to have several options for pain relief and a staff of trained personnel ready in the event of an emergency.*

As you read, consider the following questions:

1. According to the authors, what percentage of women in the United States give birth in a hospital?
2. What do the authors state is the relationship between hospital size and epidural use during labor and delivery?

3. What are some pain-management alternatives being offered to women in hospitals of all sizes?

Your choice of birth environment is the first decision you make that determines your pain-relief options. If you know you want to use modern medical pain-relief methods, you will need to select a birth environment that can accommodate these preferences. If you are leaning more toward a natural childbirth, but would like to keep your options open, you may want to be in a birth environment that offers not only nonmedical forms of pain relief but also allows accessibility to medical pain relief, should you change your mind during labor. If you are committed to using no medical pain-relief options and do not want to be in an environment where they are frequently used, you will need to choose a birth environment that has both the physical amenities and supportive caregivers you will need to successfully give birth free of any medications, using complementary and alternative pain-management techniques.

The staff of *caregivers* available to you during labor and birth can also directly impact your pain-relief options. For instance, if you think you prefer to use an epidural but are in a hospital where the only anesthesiologist is on another unit at the time when you are in need of pain relief, this can significantly impact your birth experience. Conversely, if you prefer to delay or avoid the use of medications, a busy hospital with a high percentage of epidural usage may not be the ideal environment for you to achieve this goal.

Your birth environment and the people caring for you during your labor and delivery can dramatically impact how you will perceive your childbirth experience. By choosing the type of birth environment best for you, you are more likely to feel relaxed and comfortable when you arrive and throughout the rest of your labor and birth. If you are giving birth in the setting you desire, surrounded by people who are able to meet

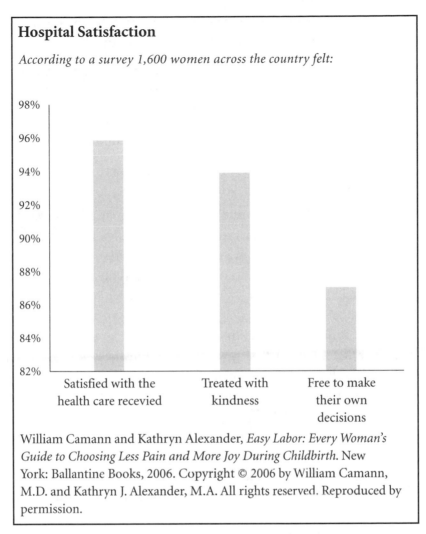

Hospital Satisfaction

According to a survey 1,600 women across the country felt:

your needs, including your pain-management needs, you are more likely to have a satisfying "birthday. . . ."

Reasons for Choosing a Hospital Birth

Most women in the United States (approximately 98 percent) give birth in a hospital. But all hospitals are not alike, and maternity units vary greatly from hospital to hospital. In addition, the size of the hospital and its maternity unit can impact the type of birth experience you have.

- You want to be in a place where all or most medical pain-relief options will be available to you.

- You want to give birth in a setting that has equipment and staff ready to deal with an unlikely emergency.

- You feel more confident in a birth environment surrounded by a variety of medical professionals.

- You want a two- to four-day recovery period before returning home with your new baby.

Larger hospitals typically offer more medical pain-management options than are found in smaller (community) hospitals. Larger hospitals are more likely to have an in-house, around-the-clock anesthesiology staff readily available if you are in need of an epidural. Often, these larger hospitals have anesthesiologists who are assigned *specifically* to the maternity unit. This reduces the likelihood of delays for women in need of pain relief that must be given by the anesthesiologist.

Smaller hospitals may not have as many medical pain-relief options and may not offer epidurals twenty-four hours a day, seven days a week. If they have a limited anesthesia staff, some smaller hospitals may not offer epidurals at all. On the other hand, many of these small hospitals, as a result of not having as much "high-tech" pain relief to offer, often have staff and equipment that can successfully support the mom who prefers to use fewer or no medications throughout labor and birth. So, depending upon your own preferences, either of these settings may be right for you. But, clearly, if you desire the full-throttle pain relief of an epidural, you are more likely to find this type of pain management taking place in larger hospitals with busier maternity units.

Managing Pain and Promoting Comfort

- In hospitals that deliver fifteen hundred or more babies per year, 69 percent of women use an epidural or a combined spinal-epidural.

- In hospitals that deliver five hundred to fifteen hundred babies per year, 50 percent of women use an epidural or a combined spinal-epidural.

- In hospitals that deliver less than five hundred babies per year, 40 percent of women use an epidural or combined spinal-epidural.

Hospitals of all sizes are increasingly responding to women's requests for more pain-management options, including baths, showers, the use of birth balls, and the promotion of movement and positioning during labor and birth. More hospitals are encouraging, or at the very least accepting, women's choice to use doulas ... as their primary support people during their labor and birth.

Many hospitals throughout the country have made their birthing rooms more appealing and homelike, with the goal of helping women feel relaxed and comfortable in the unfamiliar and sometimes intimidating surroundings of a clinical setting. Even with these changes, the hospital stay (which, for most women, is their very *first* hospital stay) can make you feel like, well, like you're in a hospital! Many caregivers recommend you bring your own homelike objects of comfort that will promote a sense of familiarity and relaxation in an otherwise unfamiliar setting. You may want to bring your favorite pillow, fragrance, photos, and a radio or CD player to listen to your favorite music. If you feel more comfy in your own clothing, let the hospital staff know you would like to wear your own threads instead of their hospital gown.

Choosing a Doctor and Hospital

Two more factors may also determine where you ultimately give birth: your insurance coverage, which may or may not cover your care at your preferred hospital, and your obstetrician's hospital affiliation. The hospital in which your obstetrician or midwife works will be the hospital where you will have your baby. If you like your obstetrician or midwife, but do not like the hospital with which he or she is affiliated, you may find you will need to switch to a doctor or midwife who works in the hospital where you want to have your baby.

"In spite of all the advertising touting 'home-like' birthing rooms in hospitals, for most women, a hospital birth will be nothing like a home birth."

Hospital Births Involve Unnecessary and Unsafe Procedures

Yvonne Cryns

Yvonne Cryns is a certified midwife and a childbirth advocate. In the following viewpoint, she argues that there are many risks to giving birth in a hospital. Despite recent attempts to make hospital births more personalized, Cryns asserts that women are still forced to lie on their backs and remain immobile throughout the labor and delivery. Also, she notes that many unnecessary and potentially harmful procedures are used in the hospital setting, such as mandatory intravenous drips, electronic fetal monitoring, and labor induction.

As you read, consider the following questions:

1. What is the window of error that Cryns identifies for ultrasounds performed in the first trimester?

2. What percentage of women who undergo cesarean section receive general anesthesia, according to the author?

3. How does Cryns describe lithotomy?

In spite of all the advertising touting "home-like" birthing rooms in hospitals, for most women, a hospital birth will be nothing like a home birth. Interventions are routine in the hospitals in my state. Every laboring woman will be hooked up for some period of time to an electronic fetal monitor, given vaginal exams, and be told where and in what position she must give birth. If her membranes are ruptured, she will be required to deliver her baby within a certain time period. If her labor is moving too slowly, she will be given Pitocin to augment it or have her water artificially ruptured. She will be told how many companions she may have with her. If she has other children, she may or may not include them at the birth. How long she is kept in the hospital will vary depending on her physician and the particular hospital. How soon her baby will be released also will depend on the baby's pediatrician and hospital policy. Some of the more common interventions that take place during hospital births are discussed below. . . .

Immobility

Along with the lithotomy position [lying on one's back with bent knees] comes immobility. It is impossible to move around when you are flat on your back. It's even more difficult if you have internal and external fetal monitors attached to your body, an IV running into your arm and after a narcotic drug was given to "take the edge off." It goes without saying, that if you had an epidural, you would not be going anywhere at all as your legs would have no feeling.

Some hospitals encourage walking and moving around. Others do not like you to be out of your room, which may be quite small and loaded with equipment, making any real walking about nearly impossible. Studies have shown that moving about and being upright can shorten labor as well as changing positions.

Induction

According to statistics from the health department in Wisconsin, one-third of all births in that state are the result of induction, the artificial starting of labor. Most inductions are accomplished using Pitocin in an intravenous solution or artificially rupturing the amniotic sac. The reasons for doing this are many. One of the most common for healthy full-term women is fear of going too far past the "due date" and having a baby with postmature syndrome or meconium staining. Another reason is fear of having a big baby.

Benefits of inducing would seem to be avoiding postmature syndrome, attempting to deliver a baby that had grown too big for the mother and bypassing meconium staining. However, studies fail to confirm this line of thought. The actual amount of time needed for a baby to grow to term varies and figuring an exact due date for each baby has not yet been done. Ultrasounds have at best a 10 day window of error if done in the first trimester. The phenomenon of postdates is poorly understood. Macrosomia occurs prior to postdates as does "postmature syndrome." The entity of postmature syndrome is based on a single physician's "subjective evaluation of 37 babies." Research seems to indicate that watchful waiting is the more prudent course of action for healthy women.

Intravenous Needles

At a great many U.S. institutions, one of the first items of care to be rendered to the obstetric patient will be her IV, "just in case." Just in case she needs drugs or surgery or her veins collapse, making insertion of an IV impossible. Nancy Wainer Cohen and Lois Estner interviewed many labor and delivery nurses to find out how frequently a laboring woman's veins

Choosing a Hospital: Questions to Ask

- Is the hospital easy to get to?

- How is it equipped to handle emergencies?

- What level nursery is available? (Nurseries are rated I, II, or III—a level III neonatal intensive care unit [NICU] is equipped to handle any neonatal emergency. A lower rating may require transportation to a level III NICU.)

- How many deliveries take place at the hospital each year? (A higher number means the hospital has more experience with various birth scenarios.)

- What is the nurse-to-patient ratio? (A ratio of 1:2 is considered good during low-risk labor; a 1:1 ratio is best in complicated cases or during the pushing stage.)

- What are the hospital's statistics for cesarean sections, episiotomies, and mortality?. . .

- How many labor and support people may be present for the birth?

- What procedures are followed after your baby's birth? Can you breastfeed immediately if desired? Is rooming-in available?

- How long is the typical postpartum stay for vaginal deliveries? For cesarean sections?

- Can the baby and the father stay with you in your room around the clock, if you desire?

"Birthing Centers and Hospital Maternity Services,"
Kids Health, www.kidshealth.org.

collapsed. They learned that this does not happen. This is not the way birth happens in other nations, where a laboring woman is permitted to eat and drink lightly. This cultural warping began in the 1940s when anesthesia was being given to nearly all birthing women by mask and vomiting and food aspiration were risks associated with this. Eliminating food and drink, they felt, would eliminate this risk. Today, however, anesthesia methods have improved and this is no longer the problem it once was. Improved intubation techniques make this problem virtually a thing of the past. Doris Haire, a maternity care writer, in looking at 20 years of medical literature on aspiration during surgery, found that the cause was not eating or drinking prior to the surgery, but caused by incompetence of the anesthesiologist.

General anesthesia is given to approximately 4% of those who undergo cesarean section. Approximately 0.3% cesarean surgeries will require intubation that will be difficult to do yet not all women who require intubation will aspirate. This translates into denying all laboring women food and drink because one cesarean sectioned woman out of 10,000 may aspirate.

Although IVs are supposed to keep the stomach empty, a glucose IV actually works to slow down the emptying of the stomach. It also may encourage tissues to swell so that it makes it more difficult to intubate, if that becomes necessary. IV fluid accumulates in the bladder and that may slow down labor. Some women may have sensitivities to the IV and have a reaction from one. It restricts the woman's mobility. The needle in the arm is painful and inhibits free movement. The baby also may suffer from the mother's IV, as studies are being done to determine if the excessive sugar administered through a glucose IV may harm the baby.

Lithotomy

This used to be the position of choice for physicians doing hospital births. The mother lies flat on her back with her knees in the air. It is a most unphysiologic position for mom and baby, but it does give the physician a good view of the mother's perineum. While in this position, the mother must push the baby out uphill. It is known to cause fetal distress due to the baby lying on the mother's arteries and veins. Most women will not choose this position if given alternatives.

Dr. Roberto Caldeyro-Barcia is considered an expert on this position for labor and delivery. He and his researchers found that this lithotomy or supine position is the worst one for laboring women because it adversely affects every facet of birth: makes labor more painful, reduces uterine activity, and can dangerously lower blood pressure. He says, "Except for being hanged by the feet, the supine position is the worst conceivable position for labor and delivery."

Monitoring

Electronic fetal monitoring [EFM] is required at nearly every hospital for at least a short time. When it was first available, it was used only for the most high risk situations. However, it is now used for everyone regardless of risk status. A large reason why EFM is used so extensively is that staff is in short supply and this technology allows for fewer care-givers.

There are two kinds of monitors: external and internal. The external monitors are attached to a heavy elastic band that is strapped across the mother's abdomen. She must lie quietly so the monitors do not slip. The baby's heart beat is recorded on a machine that documents the moment to moment heart rate on graph paper along with the mother's contractions. The internal monitor does the same things, but it is attached directly into the baby's head by a metal screw. The uterine contractions are monitored by a probe that is inserted into the uterus. Some feel that this is a more accurate reading.

During most labors and deliveries, no other method of monitoring the baby's heart rate will be used. However, EFM does not reduce infant deaths, improve outcomes, or give information that permits potentially bad situations to be corrected or avoided. The strips are frequently misread. One study found that 71–95% of babies diagnosed by EFM as distressed were not. Additionally, studies have shown that most causes of brain damage are not related to actual distress during the birth process but rather due to distress prior to labor. In spite of near universal use of EFM, little evidence exists that any change has taken place in the numbers of brain damaged babies being born.

Auscultation with a feta scope, stethoscope, pinard horn and other low-tech devices for listening to the baby have been found to be as effective for monitoring most laboring women.

The risks of using EFM are well known: higher intervention rate of all kinds due to misinterpretation of strips leading to a misdiagnosis of fetal distress. The use of EFM may increase the risk of cerebral palsy by increasing the risk of infection. More babies have abnormal fetal heart rate patterns when monitored by EFM than by auscultation, and it may be that this finding is caused by EFM rather than simply being detected by it. Mothers may report not remembering parts of their labors due to anxiety that was created by using the monitors.

Periodical Bibliography

The following articles have been selected to supplement the diverse views presented in this chapter.

Melissa J. Cheyney	"Homebirth as Systems-Challenging Praxis: Knowledge, Power, and Intimacy in the Birthplace," *Qualitative Health Research*, vol. 18, no. 2, February 2008.
Irish Times	"Should Home Be Where the Birth Is?" February 22, 2008.
Claudia Kalb	"New Childbirth Technology Tanks: A Childbirth Technology Disappoints," *Newsweek*, November 22, 2006.
Robb Kightley	"Delivering Choice: Where to Birth?" *British Journal of Midwifery*, vol. 15, no. 8, August 2007.
Julia Magill-Cuerden	"Hospital Birth, the Environment and Social Networking," *British Journal of Midwifery*, vol. 15, no. 12, December 2007.
Belleruth Naparstek	"Guided Imagery: A Best Practice for Pregnancy and Childbirth," *International Journal of Childbirth Education*, vol. 22, no. 4, September 2007.
Debby Titlebaum Neuman	"Bringing Homebirth into the Hospital," *Mothering*, March/April 2007.
Lesley Page and Jim Drife	"Do We Have Enough Evidence to Judge Midwife Led Maternity Units Safe?" *British Medical Journal*, vol. 335, no. 7621, September 29, 2007.
Michael Robertson	"'You Want to Give Birth Where?'" *Mothering*, January/February 2007.
Sarah-Kate Templeton	"All Expectant Mothers To Be Offered Home Birth Despite Risks," *The Sunday Times*, September 23, 2007.
The Times	"Home Birth Risks," April 2, 2008.

OPPOSING
VIEWPOINTS®
SERIES

CHAPTER 3

How Can Rights and Preferences Be Honored During Childbirth?

Chapter Preface

Pregnant women's bodies are constantly under social sur-
veillance. Most pregnant women have been given unsolic-
ited suggestions about nutrition and behavior. Generally, these
warnings are given out of concern for the expectant mother
and her unborn child. After all, few people would want harm
to come to a new life. Nonetheless, some pregnant women
grow weary of hearing about what they should or should not
eat, how much they should weigh, and whether they should
stop exercising. While this informal advice can easily be ignored, it is much more difficult for expectant mothers to dis-
miss the recommendations given to them by their physicians,
especially when laws exist to enforce them.

Doctors are given great authority in Western culture. After
all, they go to school for many years to gain expertise. It is no
wonder, then, that when a woman is advised by her obstetrician to go on bed rest during the remaining months of her
pregnancy, she often heeds his or her counsel. In situations
where a pregnant woman has opted not to follow her doctor's
orders, the courts have, in several cases, upheld physicians'
rights to order pregnant women to do what is in the best interest of unborn children. *Whitner v. The State of South Carolina* is perhaps the most groundbreaking of such cases. In it,
the Supreme Court of South Carolina ruled that a pregnant
woman could be charged under child abuse laws for causing
harm to her fetus following the 1992 arrest and imprisonment
of Cornelia Whitner for smoking crack cocaine while she was
pregnant.

Despite the potential need for legally sanctioned intervention, some women's health advocates argue that some of these
laws go too far. Beyond protecting unborn children, some recent court rulings seem to infringe on the Constitutional
rights of pregnant women. In *Policing Pregnancy: The Law and*

Ethics of Obstetric Conflict, Sheena Meredith reports that the consequences of such a law can radically impact women's health and their rights. She gives examples of the fallout of *Whitner v. State*: "In New Jersey, one woman was charged with neglect for using codeine for pain relief during labor, while another was threatened with losing custody of her baby for following a drug treatment program using medically prescribed methadone."

As the authors in the following chapter demonstrate, finding the best possible balance between pregnant women's rights and the health and well-being of their unborn children is not simple. Any time a human life is potentially at risk, strong opinions are to be expected.

| "We must ensure that all childbearing women ... understand and have opportunities to exercise their right to make health care decisions."

Childbearing Women Have Rights

Childbirth Connection

Childbirth Connection is a national not-for-profit organization that uses research, education, and advocacy to improve maternity care for all women and their families. In the following viewpoint, members of the group argue that childbearing women are often unaware of their rights when it comes to medical treatment during pregnancy, labor, and delivery. To raise awareness about this issue, they have assembled a list of twenty rights to which they think all pregnant women should be entitled. In addition, they assert that women whose rights have been violated must have access to various types of legal and other remedies to address their concerns.

As you read, consider the following questions:

1. Is it a legal right for a woman to receive almost all of her maternity care from a single caregiver or small group of caregivers?

2. Of the twenty rights listed in this viewpoint, which one has been challenged in courts of law?

3. Do childbearing women currently have the legal right to unrestricted access to their medical records?

This statement was developed in response to serious and continuing problems with maternity care in the United States, including:

The United States is the only wealthy industrialized nation that does not guarantee access to essential health care for all pregnant women and infants. Many women, especially those with low incomes, lack access to adequate maternity care.

A large body of scientific research shows that many widely used maternity care practices that involve risk and discomfort are of no benefit to low-risk women and infants. On the other hand, some practices that clearly offer important benefits are not widely available in U.S. hospitals.

Many women do not receive adequate information about benefits and risks of specific procedures, drugs, tests and treatments, or about alternatives.

Childbearing women frequently are not aware of their legal right to make health care choices on behalf of themselves and their babies, and do not exercise this right.

We must ensure that all childbearing women have access to information and care that is based on the best scientific evidence now available, and that they understand and have opportunities to exercise their right to make health care decisions. Women whose rights are violated need access to legal or other recourse to address their grievances.

Every Woman's Rights

Consideration and respect for every woman under all circumstances is the foundation of this statement of rights, developed by Childbirth Connection.

1. Every woman has the right to health care before, during and after pregnancy and childbirth.

> # A Declaration of the Rights of Childbearing Women
>
> Qualities inherent in safe, loving childbearing experiences must be recognized as the global rights of all women. Dangerous, dehumanizing medical procedures are violations against women's most basic human rights, and are also violations of children's rights to be born without undue pain and exploitation.
>
> Birth's integrity diminishes as obstetric interventions multiply. The rights of women and babies must be recognized.
>
> *Leilah McCracken,*
> *"A Declaration of the Rights of Childbearing Women,"*
> Midwifery Today, *Issue 50, Summer 1999.*

2. Every woman and infant has the right to receive care that is consistent with current scientific evidence about benefits and risks. Practices that have been found to be safe and beneficial should be used when indicated. Harmful, ineffective, or unnecessary practices should be avoided. Unproven interventions should be used only in the context of research to evaluate their effects.

3. Every woman has the right to choose a midwife or a physician as her maternity care provider. Both caregivers skilled in normal childbearing and caregivers skilled in complications are needed to ensure quality care for all.

4. Every woman has the right to choose her birth setting from the full range of safe options available in her community, on the basis of complete, objective information about benefits, risks and costs of these options.

5. Every woman has the right to receive all or most of her maternity care from a single caregiver or a small group of car-

egivers with whom she can establish a relationship. Every woman has the right to leave her maternity caregiver and select another if she becomes dissatisfied with her care. (Only second sentence is a legal right.)

6. Every woman has the right to information about the professional identity and qualifications of those involved with her care, and to know when those involved are trainees.

7. Every woman has the right to communicate with caregivers and receive all care in privacy, which may involve excluding nonessential personnel. She also has the right to have all personal information treated according to standards of confidentiality.

8. Every woman has the right to receive maternity care that identifies and addresses social and behavioral factors that affect her health and that of her baby. She should receive information to help her take the best care of herself and her baby and have access to social services and behavioral change programs that could contribute to their health.

9. Every woman has the right to full and clear information about benefits, risks and costs of the procedures, drugs, tests and treatments offered to her, and of all other reasonable options, including nonintervention. She should receive this information about all interventions that are likely to be offered during labor and birth well before the onset of labor.

10. Every woman has the right to accept or refuse procedures, drugs, tests and treatments, and to have her choices honored. She has the right to change her mind. (Please note that this established legal right has been challenged in a number of recent cases.)

11. Every woman has the right to be informed if her caregivers wish to enroll her or her infant in a research study. She should receive full information about all known and possible benefits and risks of participation; and she has the right to decide whether to participate, free from coercion and without negative consequences.

12. Every woman has the right to unrestricted access to all available records about her pregnancy, labor, birth, postpartum course and infant; to obtain a full copy of these records; and to receive help in understanding them, if necessary.

13. Every woman has the right to receive maternity care that is appropriate to her cultural and religious background, and to receive information in a language in which she can communicate.

14. Every woman has the right to have family members and friends of her choice present during all aspects of her maternity care.

15. Every woman has the right to receive continuous social, emotional and physical support during labor and birth from a caregiver who has been trained in labor support.

16. Every woman has the right to receive full advance information about risks and benefits of all reasonably available methods for relieving pain during labor and birth, including methods that do not require the use of drugs. She has the right to choose which methods will be used and to change her mind at any time.

17. Every woman has the right to freedom of movement during labor, unencumbered by tubes, wires or other apparatus. She also has the right to give birth in the position of her choice.

18. Every woman has the right to virtually uninterrupted contact with her newborn from the moment of birth, as long as she and her baby are healthy and do not need care that requires separation.

19. Every woman has the right to receive complete information about the benefits of breastfeeding well in advance of labor, to refuse supplemental bottles and other actions that interfere with breastfeeding, and to have access to skilled lactation support for as long as she chooses to breastfeed.

20. Every woman has the right to decide collaboratively with caregivers when she and her baby will leave the birth site for home, based on their conditions and circumstances.

> *"Many cases of cerebral palsy can be prevented through the judicious use of electronic fetal monitoring."*

Fetal Monitoring During Labor Can Prevent Cerebral Palsy and Therefore Should Be Used

Howard A. Janet

Howard A. Janet, a lawyer for the firm Janet, Jenner, and Suggs, focuses on birth injury litigation. In the following viewpoint, he argues that because electronic fetal monitoring (EFM) during labor and delivery can prevent cerebral palsy it should be a routine part of the childbirth experience. Using current medical research, he debunks many myths surrounding the use of EFM and encourages parents to better understand EFM procedures and data.

As you read, consider the following questions:

1. According to Dr. Joseph J. Volpe, what percentage of children with cerebral palsy develop the condition from intrapartum asphyxia?
2. In the author's estimation, how has the number of children with cerebral palsy changed over the years?
3. What percentage of all labor and delivery rooms in the United States use electronic fetal monitoring, according to Janet?

Parents must realize that their quest foreknowledge about their children's health care should start before the labor and delivery process. When you undertake your research, you will be astounded by the misinformation you will find. For instance:

Rates of Cerebral Palsy

Misinformation: Children rarely develop CP [cerebral palsy][1] from asphyxial injuries to the brain during the intrapartum [labor and delivery] period. The American College of Obstetricians and Gynecologists [ACOG] claims that several studies support the conclusion that only four percent of CP results solely from asphyxia during labor.

Reality: The studies on which ACOG relies are inferior and unreliable. Even if the scope of the inquiry were limited to instances of CP where intrapartum asphyxia is the sole cause as opposed to the primary cause, the actual percentage would be approximately three times greater. According to Joseph J. Volpe, M.D., Harvard professor and neurologist-in-chief at Boston's Children's Hospital, if all term infants are considered, the percentage of children who develop CP from intrapartum asphyxia is "approximately 12 to 23 percent" which equates to "a large absolute number of infants." Dr. Volpe concludes, fur-

1. Cerebral palsy is an incurable condition in which a part of the brain, the cerebrum, has been damaged. The condition causes physical disability and motor disorders.

ther, that the "tendency in the medical profession to deny the importance or even the existence of intrapartum brain injury" is "particularly unfortunate," and may well be impairing progress in CP prevention.

The Role of Electronic Fetal Monitoring

Misinformation: Electronic fetal monitoring [EFM] has not reduced the number of children who develop cerebral palsy.

Reality: This false claim fails to take into account today's enhanced survival rates of premature infants. Nationally renowned maternal-fetal medicine specialist Richard H. Paul, M.D., who is one of the pioneers in EFM, and other experts have testified to the inaccuracy of this claim in malpractice trials brought by parents who contend that their children's cerebral palsy was caused by medical error.

In the days before EFM and recent medical advancements, doctors lacked the expertise and technology to save many premature babies; generally, efforts made to save infants weighing less than three pounds were tragically unsuccessful. Today, infants of a pound or less receive active treatment and life support, and routinely survive. These premature infants represent a substantial number of the children born with CP. Yet, despite the addition of these preemies to the survival pool, the total number of infants born with CP has remained constant.

If the number of surviving premature babies who develop CP has significantly increased, but the total number of cases of CP remains the same, then the number of full-term infants that have CP must have declined. Many infants who otherwise might have developed CP have escaped an unfortunate fate because EFM was used properly during labor and delivery.

Interpreting EFM Patterns

Misinformation: Obstetricians disagree so widely in their interpretation of EFM tracings that standards for interpretation and appropriate action in response to a particular EFM pattern do not exist except in the face of tracings that are perfectly normal or extremely and obviously abnormal. This contention is primarily based on three studies.

Reality: These studies are unpersuasive and outdated, with one being more than 23 years old and each involving no more than five obstetricians. For many years, highly qualified obstetricians from all over the country have testified in medical malpractice cases that standards of care indeed do exist for the interpretation and management of various EFM tracing patterns that fall between those two extremes.

In connection with a medical malpractice lawsuit brought by a Minnesota mother whose child developed CP as a result of intrapartum asphyxia, a medical article was uncovered that shed light on at least one reason why doctors resist establishing written standards for the interpretation and management of the so-called in between patterns. "Providers have traditionally been hesitant to codify guidelines for managing FHR [fetal heart rate] pattern tracings. The reasons commonly cited include fears that written guidelines will be used to scrutinize clinical practice in a court of law."

When EFM patterns provide evidence of impending fetal asphyxia, such patterns need not reach the extremely abnormal level before immediate action, such as expedited cesarean delivery, must be taken. Yet, because medically sanctioned literature suggests that less-than-extreme EFM tracings don't necessarily require intervention, many otherwise healthy babies sustain intrapartum brain injuries and are subsequently diagnosed with CP.

More Misguided Priorities

As much as parents would like to believe that the best interests of mother and baby are always the first priority of the doctors and nurses who treat them, unfortunately, other considerations possibly come into play. According to the Association of Women's Health, Obstetrics and Neonatal Nurses

Monitoring the Fetal Heart Rate

Auscultation [listening for sounds] of the fetal heart rate (FHR) is performed by external or internal means. External monitoring is performed using a hand-held Doppler ultrasound probe to auscultate and count the FHR during a uterine contraction and for 30 seconds thereafter to identify fetal response. It may also be performed using an external transducer, which is placed on the maternal abdomen and held in place by an elastic belt or girdle. The transducer uses Doppler ultrasound to detect fetal heart motion and is connected to an FHR monitor. The monitor calculates and records the FHR on a continuous strip of paper. Recently, second-generation fetal monitors have incorporated microprocessors and mathematic procedures to improve the FHR signal and the accuracy of the recording. Internal monitoring is performed by attaching a screw-type electrode to the fetal scalp with a connection to an FHR monitor. The fetal membranes must be ruptured, and the cervix must be at least partially dilated before the electrode may be placed on the fetal scalp.

Amir Sweha, Trevor W. Hacker, and Jim Nuovo,
"Interpretation of the Electronic Fetal Heart Rate During Labor,"
American Academy of Family Physicians, May 1, 1999.

(AWHONN), nurses may hesitate to document a physician's conduct in the medical record for fear those notes will end up in the courtroom: "[Nurses] are usually told by risk management personnel not to 'advertise' potential conflicts in the medical records and thus some nurses may be unwilling to memorialize an unsuccessful interaction with a physician. Nurses may choose to affirmatively protect the doctor by not documenting an inappropriate or untimely response in the patient's chart."

Once parents like you learn that even a publication of a professional nursing organization notes that its members are cautioned against documenting potential medical errors, you will realize the gravity of this matter and the importance of researching these issues.

A Call to Action

Significant numbers of highly qualified, respected physicians have concluded that many cases of cerebral palsy can be prevented through the judicious use of electronic fetal monitoring. Their position is supported by recent medical studies that have established a distinct relationship between certain fetal heart rate patterns and poor neurological outcomes in infants up to a year after birth.

And while there may be no universally agreed upon set of terms to describe actionable EFM pattern characteristics, it is clear that doctors know a great deal about the patterns that foreshadow CP and other poor neonatal outcomes. By using EFM in 85 percent of all labor and delivery rooms nationwide, the medical community already has acknowledged EFM's value. Now, medical leaders should take action to adopt clearcut written protocols concerning the interpretation of EFM tracings and appropriate interventions. Doing so will help reduce the number of errors made in connection with interpreting and responding to EFM tracings.

Health care organizations that promote better patient care should develop formalized classes and seminars that focus not only on easing the mother's pain, but also on educating parents-to-be about EFM and other matters that will help them to be proactive in their health care.

These are complex, technical subjects, and some may be difficult to research, but accurate information is available. There really are standards, even if they have not been reduced to writing or codified by the obstetrical community. You, as parents, must do the research necessary to learn more about EFM and its value in the labor and delivery rooms.

Remember, *knowledge is power.*

As I travel across the country representing parents of children with CP, I'm often asked, "Is there anything I could have done?" Second-guessing themselves only adds to the agony for these parents. I tell them, "No, there's nothing you could have done." A mother and father who have given themselves and their unborn child over to the care of professionals should never be held accountable for what happens in a labor and delivery room.

But, what they can do to help someone else avoid what happened to them—or to reduce the risk of the tragedy reoccurring in their family—is an entirely different matter. Learning a few basics of EFM is not difficult. It is imperative to recognize significant fetal heart rate decelerations (dips below the baseline rate) in the fetal monitor tracings. You must also understand the relationship of decelerations to contractions. Isolated decelerations of short duration (less than 30 seconds) generally are thought to be inconsequential. However, if certain types of decelerations become repetitive or prolonged, this could mean your baby is not being adequately oxygenated. You should also realize that the presence of variability (the second-to-second and longer-term jagged lines or variations in the fetal heart rate tracings) is usually reassuring. On the other hand, decreased or absent variability can be foreboding.

Armed with sufficient knowledge, you will be able to question your health care providers intelligently. Some AWHONN publications provide easily understandable information about EFM patterns. Well-founded questions will spark your health care providers to be more attentive to your care and that of your unborn baby.

Proactive Measures

Other important proactive measures that parents should take include:

- Help dispel the myth that CP rarely results from intra-partum asphyxia. It only hampers prevention efforts.

- Encourage expectant couples you know, especially those with high-risk pregnancies, to learn about EFM.

- Be sure that your health care providers have the appropriate training, certifications, and experience necessary to properly interpret fetal monitor tracings.

- Make sure your labor and delivery health care providers know you want to be informed about evidence of reduced fetal oxygenation and interventions that are being considered.

- Confirm that an obstetrician and anesthesiologist are in-house and available to respond in an emergency situation.

- Understand the chain of command in the hospital so that if you feel your concerns are being ignored you have an alternative source for an opinion and intervention.

The message for parents-to-be: Get proactive about your pregnancy and delivery. Move past the curriculum of Lamaze classes. Learn about more than how your baby is developing in the womb. Educate yourselves about EFM, and learn the right questions to ask about how your baby is being monitored during labor and delivery.

Because there really is only one certainty and it is this: No one—no one—cares as much about your child as you do.

> *"After 25 years of use, electronic fetal heart-rate monitoring was associated with an unchanged rate of cerebral palsy."*

Fetal Monitoring During Labor Cannot Prevent Cerebral Palsy and Therefore Should Not Be Used

Michael F. Greene

Michael F. Greene practices maternal and fetal medicine and obstetrics and gynecology in Boston, Massachusetts. In the following viewpoint, he states that medical care providers adopted the routine use of electronic fetal heart-rate monitors before it could be proved that they were successful in determining certain fetal distress. He points to recent studies which have shown that such devices are not capable of preventing cerebral palsy as once was believed. Greene encourages other physicians to carefully consider the use of technology when treating patients because untested practices can lead to potentially destructive consequences, such as higher rates of cesarean sections.

Michael F. Greene, "Obstetricians Still Await a Deus ex Machina," *The New England Journal of Medicine*, vol. 335, no. 21, November 23, 2006, pp. 2247–2248. Copyright © 2006 Massachusetts Medical Society. All rights reserved. Reproduced by permission.

As you read, consider the following questions:

1. As Greene explains, by the end of what decade had fetal heart-rate monitoring become a routine part of care during labor and delivery?

2. How often is the cause of cerebral palsy known, according to the author?

3. Why was fetal pulse oximetry developed, according to Greene?

Intrapartum [during labor and delivery] electronic fetal heart-rate monitoring was introduced with great enthusiasm in the early 1970s. Most cases of cerebral palsy were thought to result from asphyxia during the intrapartum period, and it was hoped that the ability to recognize intrapartum fetal asphyxia and intervene with a timely delivery would reduce the incidence of fetal neurologic injury. During the years after the adoption of electronic fetal monitoring, numerous publications documented associations between various fetal heart-rate patterns and short-term outcome measures of neonatal well-being. These outcome measures were assumed to be reliable surrogates for the development of long-term neurologic handicaps. By the end of the 1970s, electronic fetal heart-rate monitoring had become a standard of care, despite the absence of randomized, controlled trials showing any reduction in the rate of long-term neurologic handicaps in the newborns.

When electronic fetal monitoring was rigorously assessed, however, the results provided little support for its use. Initial trials that showed no benefit from intrapartum monitoring were criticized for their small size. Larger trials that showed no benefit, including one involving almost 35,000 patients,[1] were criticized because they were conducted in term infants

1. Levano KJ, Cunningham FG, Nelson S, et al. A prospective comparison of selective and universal electronic fetal monitoring in 34,995 pregnancies, N Enghl J Med 1986;315:615–9.

who were at low risk. A study reported in the *Journal* in 1990 showed no significant differences in the results of neurologic evaluations at 18 months of age among premature infants at high risk for intrapartum asphyxia who were randomly assigned to electronic monitoring and those assigned to intermittent auscultation during labor.[2] The accompanying editorial characterized intrapartum fetal monitoring as "a disappointing story."[3]

Where had we gone wrong? First, our basic premise was flawed. Only a small fraction of all cases of cerebral palsy arise from known causes, and a small fraction of those from intrapartum asphyxia.[4] Although electronic fetal heart-rate monitoring is technically easy to implement, interpretation of the data is subjective, difficult to standardize, and poorly reproducible. Experienced observers often disagree with one another's interpretations of monitoring records, and when asked to reexamine those same records months later, they frequently disagree with their own original interpretations.[5] Abnormal fetal heart-rate patterns observed during labor may reflect preexisting neurologic injury of the fetus that cannot be ameliorated by intrapartum interventions. Finally, a nonreassuring fetal heart-rate pattern should be seen as an imperfect screening test for fetal asphyxia, rather than as a diagnostic test for asphyxia.

After 25 years of use, electronic fetal heart-rate monitoring was associated with an unchanged rate of cerebral palsy in term infants but a soaring rate of cesarean deliveries.[6] Simul-

2. Shy KK, Luthy DA, Bennett FC, et al. Effects of electronic fetal-heart-rate monitoring, as compared with periodic auscultation, on the neurologic development of premature infants. N Engl J Med 1990;322;588–93.
3. Freeman R. Intrapartum fetal monitoring—a disappointing story. N Enghl J Med 1990;322;624–6.
4. Nelson KB. Can we prevent cerebral palsy? N Engl J Med 2003;349;1765–9.
5. Trimbos JB, Keirse MJ. Observer variability in assessment of antepartum cardiotocograms. Br J Obstet Gynaecol 1978;85: 900–6.
6. Clark SL, Hankins GDV. Temporal and demographic trends in cerebral palsy—fact and fiction. Am J Obstet Gynecol 2003;188:628–33.

taneously, lawsuits alleging neonatal neurologic injury due to failure to diagnose and effectively treat intrapartum asphyxia were increasing. Although the precise fractional contributions to the rising rate of cesarean deliveries that were performed for presumed fetal asphyxia (as opposed to fear of potential litigation) are debatable and difficult to quantify, they are real and substantial.

Because of the limitations of fetal heart-rate monitoring, technology was developed for continuous measurement of fetal oxygen saturation during labor, with the goal of more accurately assessing fetal well-being and reducing the number of unnecessary cesarean deliveries. A randomized, controlled trial showed that the technical ability of fetal pulse oximetry to obtain data about fetal oxygen saturation safely, fairly reliably, and with minimal discomfort was acceptable to most women in labor.[7] Despite a reduction in the rate of cesarean deliveries that were performed out of concern for intrapartum asphyxia, the overall rate of cesarean deliveries in the monitored group was undiminished, owing to an increase in the rate of cesarean deliveries performed for the indication of dystocia.[8] Subsequently, other studies have replicated these findings but failed to provide any real insight into the association between nonreassuring fetal heart-rate patterns and dystocia.[8,9]

In this issue of the *Journal*, Bloom et al.[10] report the results of the largest trial to date of this relatively new technology. Salient entry criteria for study subjects were the presence of labor at term with an apparently normal singleton fetus in

7. Garite TJ, Dildy GA, McNamara H, et al. A multicenter controlled trial of fetal pulse oximetry in the intrapartum management of nonreassuring fetal heart rate patterns. AM J Obstet Gynecol 2000;183:1049–58.
8. East CE, Brennecke SP, King JF, Chan FY, Colditz PB. The effect of intrapartum fetal pulse oximetry, in the presence of a nonreassuring fetal heart rate pattern, on operative delivery rates; a multicenter, randomized, controlled trial (the FOREMOST trial). Am J Obstet Gynecol 2006;194:606.e1–606.e16.
9. Porreco RP, Boehm FH, Dildy GA, et al. Dystocia in nulliparous patients monitored with fetal pulse oximetry. Am J Obstet Gynecol 2004;190:113–7.
10. Bloom SL, Sponge CY, Thom E, et al. Fetal pulse oximetry and cesarean delivery. N Engl J Med 2006;355:2195–202.

Electronic Fetal Monitoring During Labor

At the time EFM was introduced in the 1950s, physicians felt that its use would . . . reduce the cesarean birth rate because hypoxia [a deficiency of oxygen, a possible cause of cerebral palsy] could be more accurately diagnosed. However, there has been no significant reduction in cerebral palsy since EFM was introduced and the cesarean rate in the U.S. has steadily risen.

Becky Sisk, "Electronic Fetal Monitoring During Labor," 2002.
www.enursescribe.com.

vertex presentation. All subjects underwent placement of the monitoring device, but the information from the device was hidden from care providers for half the subjects. The primary goal of monitoring with the use of fetal pulse oximetry was to reduce the overall rate of cesarean delivery. Unlike earlier studies,[7,8] study subjects were not required to have a nonreassuring fetal heart-rate pattern for enrollment, but a large, planned sample was expected to include enough patients with nonreassuring fetal heart-rate patterns to have a high probability of finding a difference in cesarean delivery rates in that subgroup if the intervention was efficacious. As with previous studies, application of the monitoring device was generally successful, was not associated with a high incidence of adverse effects, and was successful in obtaining the desired data about fetal oxygen saturation approximately 74% of the time the device was in place. Unfortunately, knowledge of this additional fetal physiological information did not change the rates of cesarean or operative vaginal delivery in either the general study population of 5341 women or the subgroup of 2168 women with no reassuring fetal heart-rate patterns. The reduction in the rate of cesarean deliveries that were performed out of concern for intrapartum fetal asphyxia seen in previous studies was not observed in this trial, nor was there the enigmatic increase in cesarean deliveries for the indication of dystocia among women with nonreassuring fetal heart-rate patterns. The performance of electronic fetal heart rate monitoring as a screening test for fetal oxygen desaturation was poor. Neonatal outcomes were not significantly different between the groups.

As noted by the authors in their discussion, fetal pulse oximetry, unlike electronic fetal heart-rate monitoring, has not been widely disseminated before appropriate trials were conducted to define the true usefulness of the new technology. This genie has not yet escaped from the bottle.[11] This case does offer the opportunity to discuss the appropriate role of the Food and Drug Administration (FDA) in approving new medical devices. Should the FDA's charge be minimalist and framed very narrowly, to approve a device that reliably does what it claims—in this case, accurately record fetal oxygen saturation—while not injuring people in the process? Or should the FDA's charge be more expansive, to approve a new device only after it demonstrates some medical value added to the current standard of care?

More than 30 years ago the new technology of electronic fetal heart-rate monitoring was introduced with the noble aspiration to eliminate cerebral palsy. We now find ourselves in the far less noble position of seeking new technology to mitigate the unintended and undesirable consequences of our last ineffective, but nonetheless persistent, technologic innovation.

---

11. Muller JE, Stone PH, Markis JE, Braunwald E. Let's not let the genie escape from the bottle—again. N Engl J Med 1981;304:1294–6.

| "The written birth plan is an important tool to help women achieve their personal goals and have the birth they want."

Birth Plans Can Improve the Childbirth Experience

Judith Lothian

Judith Lothian is a nursing professor at Seton Hall University in New Jersey. In the following viewpoint, she argues that the use of a birth plan can help women experience more satisfying births. She notes that childbirth contentment is the result of the fulfillment of the mother's personal expectations and involvement in decision making and the quality of and her relationship with caregivers. Lothian asserts that all of these conditions can be met by respecting the mother's birth plan when safety permits.

As you read, consider the following questions:

1. In the author's opinion, how do expectations about childbirth affect women's satisfaction with their births?

2. What are the two main views about the childbirth process that Lothian identifies?

Judith Lothian, "Birth Plans: The Good, the Bad, and the Future," *Journal of Obstetric, Gynecologic, and Neonatal Nursing*, vol. 35, no. 2, 2006, pp. 295, 297–300, 302. Copyright © 2006. AWHONN, The Association of Women's Health, Obstetric and Neonatal Nurses. Reproduced by permission of Blackwell Publishers.

3. According to Lothian, what are four interventions regularly used by hospital staff during labor and birth?

The written birth plan was introduced in the 1980s, in an increasingly medicalized maternity environment, as a tool to help women clarify their desires and communicate these to their caregivers. Today, intervention-intensive birth is the norm, and birth plans are as likely to reflect a desire for interventions, including epidural, elective induction, and cesarean, as they are to express women's desire to avoid unnecessary interventions. The tension caused by birth plans reflects the larger problems with contemporary maternity care: conflicting beliefs about birth and what constitutes safe, effective care. At the heart of the debate are ethical issues related to informed consent and informed refusal. This article will attempt to untangle the issues and propose new ways of thinking about, developing, and using birth plans. . . .

The Purpose of the Birth Plan

Birth is an important part of a woman's life, not just another day. A satisfying birth will have a lasting positive effect, just as a traumatic or unsatisfying experience will have negative one. Creating a birth plan provides the opportunity to determine personal expectations, develop relationships with providers, and share in decision making—critical components in achieving a satisfying birth experience. Contrary to what women may think before going into labor, the amount of pain they experience does not influence women's satisfaction with birth. Four factors do influence satisfaction: personal expectations, the amount of support from caregivers, the quality of the caregiver-patient relationship, and involvement in decision making. Each of these can be facilitated by a birth plan.

Determining Personal Expectations: A woman's plan for her birth is a reflection of her personal story: her dreams and aspirations, her fears, worries, and concerns. Women report that making a birth plan encourages them to think about choices and what kind of birth they want, and to become acquainted with available options before labor begins. High expectations seem to increase the likelihood of a positive birth experience, whereas women with low expectations tend to be less satisfied with their births. Women have reported that writing a birth plan provides the opportunity to discuss their feelings and thoughts with partners and begin to clarify their needs and wants with them, setting into motion the development of a strong support network.

Developing Relationships with Providers: When birth took place in communities, childbearing women were assisted by midwives or family physicians who knew them (and their families) well. In the *Listening to Mothers* survey [conducted in 2002 by the Maternity Center Association], almost one-third of the women reported that their primary birth atten-dant was not their primary provider. Ten percent had only met briefly, and 19 percent had never met their primary birth attendant. The birth plan can help nurses as well as physicians recognize women as individuals and appreciate their individu-ality more quickly. A caring but busy nurse will want to know quickly what is most important to the woman she is caring for, what she needs to feel safe, what she is fearful of, who she wants with her in labor, how she wishes to cope with her con-tractions, and what interventions she would like to avoid.

The birth plan is not intended to be simply a list of re-quests but rather a tool to facilitate communication between women and those who will care for them in labor. Communi-cation involves ongoing dialogue throughout pregnancy and during labor and birth to foster trust, respect, autonomy, and integrity of all involved. The birth plan should be a living document that reflects increased information, changing cir-cumstances, and ongoing communication.

Sharing in Decision Making: Ideally, when making personal decisions about medical care, including routine interventions, women clarify their desires and expectations, discuss alternatives, access and understand best evidence, continue discussions with their caregiver, and then make a personal decision—informed consent or informed refusal. In a less than ideal world, this process may break down for several reasons, an important one being lack of access to full, accurate information.

Birth plans are a valuable tool for promoting informed decisions. Unlike a decade ago, information about best practice is now widely available and women do not need to rely completely on their caregivers for information. Women can access the Cochrane Library, the Maternity Center Association Website, the Coalition for the Improvement of Maternity Services, and the Lamaze Institute for Normal Birth and find evidence-based information. Decisions women ultimately make may include choices that do not reflect best evidence, but if they have full, accurate information, we can have confidence that a truly informed decision has been made.

Some decisions—the kind of support women want, how they will find comfort with increasingly difficult contractions, what they need to feel safe in labor—have nothing to do with medical care. These personal preferences should be respected, but often are not due to restrictive hospital policies. For example, a woman might want more than one person with her in labor, but give birth in a hospital that has a policy of only allowing one support person, or she may be most comfortable walking but is restricted to bed by policy. [Researcher Sooi-Ken] Too described a woman' s feelings when her birth plan was ignored: "It is much more of a let down or a betrayal if it [the birth plan] is not looked at or carried out. If you are given choices and they can't grant you the requests because they don't have the time or staff, what is the point?"

Why the Tension? Two Different Views

The goals of the hospital system are often at odds with goals of an individualized birth plan. Tensions arise from conflicting beliefs about birth, choice and control, and power balance between women and their caregivers.

One view of birth is that nature has designed labor and birth simply and elegantly, and women have an inherent ability to birth their babies. An evolving body of research demonstrates the danger of interfering in the normal, natural process of labor and birth without a clear medical indication. Even a simple intervention, like restricting eating and drinking in labor, can disrupt the process, creating problems that in turn must be managed with more intervention. For this reason, the [World Health Organization] WHO recommended that the goal of maternity care be to achieve a healthy mother and child with the least intervention possible. For almost all women, labor and birth are likely to proceed safely without any medical interventions. Caregivers who believe in the wisdom of nature's plan for birth and women's ability to give birth trust the process of birth and are reluctant to intervene without clear medical indication. They are vigilant but patient. They encourage women to create personal environments in which they can feel safe and able to do the work of labor.

The alternative view is that labor and birth are risky and fraught with the possibility that things could go terribly wrong. Highlighting the riskiness of birth increases women's fears and solidifies the power of the obstetrician. If you "expect trouble," the management of labor and birth is quite different. Safety means routine intravenous lines, continuous EFM [electronic fetal monitoring], and restrictions on eating and drinking, just in case a complication arises.

In *A Guide to Effective Care in Pregnancy and Childbirth*, [Murray] Enkin et al. noted that "the only justification for practices that restrict a woman's autonomy, her freedom of choice or access to her baby would be clear evidence that these practices do more good than harm". Based on best evidence, the *routine* use of continuous EFM, intravenous fluids, restrictions on movement, and separation of mothers from their babies is not justified.

Although best evidence supports the first view of birth, nurses, like women themselves, may find themselves somewhere along the continuum, believing that nature has designed the process of birth well, but because things can and do sometimes go wrong, it makes sense to reduce risk in every way possible. Unfortunately, risk can never be totally eliminated, and in attempting to reduce risk we often increase it. The routine use of fetal monitoring was intended to reduce risk for the baby but actually increases the risk of cesarean with no benefit for the baby.

If women find themselves with caregivers and in hospitals that "expect trouble," women are unlikely to be able to shape their own experience in other than superficial ways, such as being able to listen to music but not being allowed out of bed. Unfortunately, women choose providers and places of birth early in pregnancy and rarely have the information they need to understand how powerfully these choices will impact their ability to be an active participant in designing their birth experience. The result is too often a "bad fit" that is discovered only as the labor progresses. . . .

Power Imbalance Between Women and Caregivers

[According to researchers Quinn Perry et al.,] "The fundamental problem is not so much a lack of communication as a clash of worldviews, coupled with the [obstetrician's] confidence in one's own rectitude that allows you to take advantage of a supine opponent." The power imbalance between patients and providers may be more striking in obstetrics than in other medical fields because in a biomedical worldview, precautionary measures become viewed as essential care. Patients do not often question routine medical practices like intrave-

Birth Plan for Avoiding Unnecessary Interventions

Goal	Strategy
This is what I will do to avoid routine use of EFM [electronic fetal monitoring]:	Remind myself that routine EFM does not make birth safer for my baby
	Talk to my caregiver about intermittent monitoring
	Stay at home as long as possible in labor
	Choose a caregiver and hospital that does not require EFM
This is what I will do to keep labor as normal as possible if I need EFM:	Remind myself that my body knows how to protect my baby during labor
	Continue to move as much as possible, both in the bed and out of the bed
	Ask the staff to turn off the sound
	Ask the nurse to disconnect the monitor for me to walk to the bathroom regularly
	Remind my support team that I will need even more hands-on support

Judith Lothian, "Birth Plans: The Good, the Bad, and the Future," Journal of Obstetric, Gynecology, and Neonatal Nursing, *Vol. 35, no. 2, 2006.*

nous fluid administration associated with major surgery when evidence supports their importance. In contrast, it is reasonable to question routine intravenous infusion during labor, when evidence suggests it is unlikely to be beneficial.

[R.] DeVries and [E.] Cartwright and [J.] Thomas suggested that groups gain power by offering ways to reduce risk and uncertainty. The perception of risk can be created or increased by redefining ordinary life events as risky and exaggerating smaller risks. Because the medical model of birth encourages women (and nurses) to see birth as fraught with risk for mother and baby, the obstetrician is then in the powerful position of reducing the risk and uncertainty.

How much of caregivers' or hospitals' reluctance to allow choice is related to fear of malpractice litigation? In obstetrics, legal considerations rather than best evidence often appear to direct practice. The routine use of continuous EFM increases the risk of cesarean with no benefit for the baby, and yet EFM is standard practice in many places because of the threat of litigation. Fear of litigation may not be an ethical rationale for providing care that increases risks for mother or baby, or both.

In the 1983 Monty Python comedy, *The Meaning of Life*, with birth imminent, the mother frantically asks, "What do I do?" The obstetrician's authoritative response is, "Nothing! You're not qualified!" This scene mirrors a common response when women want to have some say in the birth of their babies, but their desires challenge the status quo. Too's qualitative research provides further insight. One midwife believed that women were "incapable of making rational decisions in labor," and others commented that "it's often quicker to decide for the women than to go through the lengthy process of dialogue and negotiation to find a way for action which respected the women's wishes." Communication is an integral part of planning for birth, but it is difficult to have a dialogue when women and their caregivers hold opposing worldviews, the hospital is inflexible, and providers think they do not have time to talk. It is even harder if the power is clearly in the hands of the hospital and the provider.

The Future of Birth Plans

Considerations for Hospitals and Providers: The evidence-based practices that promote, protect, and support normal birth should be the standard in all birth settings. Routine interventions—continuous EFM, restrictions on eating and drinking, routine intravenous lines, and restrictions on movement and positioning (without clear medical indication)—compromise the safety of birth for mother and baby, but too many hospital policies do not reflect this evidence. Written birth plans are often the only means of women to protect themselves from harmful routines in units with fixed protocols for labor. Unfortunately, [as researcher Sally Inch notes,] "The units where birth plans are most welcome are also those in which the underlying approach make them least necessary."

The birth plan provides an ongoing opportunity for dialogue as decisions are made throughout pregnancy and in labor. This dialogue is an essential component in obtaining informed consent. It's not a surprise that ethicists are studying birth plans in relation to the issues of both informed consent and informed refusal. [Quinn Perry et al. states,] "We need doctors who take with deep seriousness what they (women) want even if those desires represent medical heresy." Hospitals and providers should take seriously Enkin et al.'s caution: "The only justification for practices that restrict a woman's autonomy, her freedom of choice or access to her baby would be clear evidence that these practices do more good than harm." However, when a patient does not give consent and a physician believes he/she is unable to practice safely, the medical team should be protected from prosecution if complications result from the informed refusal. If this protection was assured, would hospitals and providers be more willing to ease restrictions and allow women to have real choices in labor? These are issues that will need to be addressed. . . .

Considerations for Childbearing Women: If the birth plan is for a safe and personally satisfying birth, the focus should expand from "these are the medical interventions I do not [or do] want" to "this is what I need, in order to experience as normal and safe a birth as possible *for me* even if labor presents the unexpected."

Women should be encouraged to think about birth early in pregnancy and to choose caregivers and places of birth whose practices reflect best evidence. In order to have the birth she wants, a woman may have to consider changing caregivers or place of birth.

In labor, women need to have confidence in their ability to give birth, to have the freedom to find comfort in a wide variety of ways, and to have continuous, emotional and physical support throughout labor. In developing the birth plan, each woman should focus on these questions: What will I do to stay confident and feel safe? What will I do to find comfort in response to my contractions? Who will support me through labor and what will I need from them?. . .

With this focus, the woman rather than the caregiver or hospital takes the lead in her labor experience. Women develop a deeper understanding of how they can shape their own experience, even if the hospital is restrictive. But contingency plans should be included, in case the hospital is restrictive, circumstances change, or complications occur. . . .

The written birth plan is an important tool to help women achieve their personal goals and have the birth they want. The problem is not women's desire to shape their birth experience but rather our inability to explore their underlying worldviews, respect their aspirations, and create environments in which they can have the birth they want. Future research on the effect of birth plans should take into consideration hospital policy and practice and "the extent to which other strategies for promoting communication are being pursued," [argues Stephanie Brown and Judith Lumley of the Centre for the Study of Mother's and Children's Health in Victoria, Australia]. As maternity care becomes more evidence based, written birth plans to control unnecessary intrusions may become a relic. Until that time, women will, and should, continue their efforts to plan for their babies' births and shape a personally satisfying experience. Women will always need to plan for and communicate to their families and their caregivers what they need to feel safe, comforted, and supported in labor. Nurses must appreciate the birth plan for what it is: a woman's attempt to be cared for as an individual, to avoid intrusions, and to begin a dialogue.

| "A birth plan may form a barrier for the encounter between the midwife and the woman."

Birth Plans Do Not Improve the Childbirth Experience

Ingela Lundgren, Marie Berg, and Ginilla Lindmark

Ingela Lundgren, Marie Berg, and Gunilla Lindmark are researchers at Göteborg University in Sweden. In the following viewpoint, they discuss the results of their study, which examined the impact of birth plans on women's satisfaction of labor and delivery. While they acknowledge that there may be some limits to the application of their findings, they argue that among their study participants, having a birth plan did not make women feel more content with their childbirth experiences.

As you read, consider the following questions:

1. According to the authors, why were birth plans introduced in the 1980s?
2. How many women participated in this study?
3. Under what circumstances do the authors assert might a birth plan be unnecessary?

Ingela Lundgren, Marie Berg, and Ginilla Lindmark, "Is the Childbirth Experience Improved by a Birth Plan," *Journal of Midwifery and Women's Health*, vol. 48, no. 5, 2003, pp. 322–327. Copyright © 2003 by the American College of Nurse-Midwives. All rights reserved. Reproduced with permission from Elsevier.

The experience of childbirth is an important life event for women. The character of this experience has implications for the future well-being of the woman and the child, the relationship between mother and child, and the new family. One of the most important factors for a positive childbirth experience is the quality of the relationship between the midwife and the woman. To help women have an improved experience of childbirth, birth plans were introduced in the 1980s. A birth plan focuses on the relationship between the midwife and the woman and helps the woman to feel more in control of events and processes during childbirth by allowing options to be considered in advance and choices to be made about some of the events that might occur during childbirth.

Birth plans take a variety of formats: they may be a formatted list of events that might occur during labor, which the woman checks as acceptable, or a list with yes or no options, or a more open format with headings as prompts. [Researchers Heather M.] Whitford and [Edith M.] Hillan found that although the use of a birth plan did not affect the degree of control felt by women, most women found that the process of completion of a birth plan was valuable. According to [Sooi-Ken] Too, however, some women prefer midwives to exercise control and decision making, and a birth plan may offer meaningless choices for them. Some studies indicate that need for control, decision making, and expectations are influenced by socioeconomic status. Before childbirth, women of high socioeconomic status prioritize control and self-empowerment, in contrast to women of low socioeconomic status who prioritize a painless delivery and a healthy baby. Hence, it is possible that a birth plan would be more positive for women of higher socioeconomic status. According to one study, the capacity of a birth plan to empower the woman depends on open communication, adequate life skills, a nurturing and caring environment, and a democratic management structure. Although birth plans have been introduced to help women have an improved experience of childbirth, the numbers of studies that evaluate the effect of birth plans are limited.

The aim of the present study was to assess the effects of answering a questionnaire and formulating a birth plan at the end of pregnancy on women's experiences of childbirth. Our hypotheses were that (1) the intervention would improve women's experiences of childbirth and (2) these improvements would be dependent on socioeconomic class.

Study Setting

Maternity care during pregnancy was established in Sweden during the 1940s as part of the welfare policy and is today integrated in the general health care system. From an international perspective, Swedish maternity care is a unique example of a successful public health project, providing free-of-cost services for all women. The program offers assistance during pregnancy and through 12 weeks postpartum, and also offers optional childbirth education. When the woman is healthy and has a normal pregnancy, midwives provide all antenatal [before birth] care. During childbirth, the midwives care for women who have a normal labor and birth. When complications or risk factors occur during pregnancy or childbirth, an obstetrician takes over the responsibility, but the midwife is still involved. However, the midwives in hospitals and those in the primary health care clinics have different employers, which may lead to lack of continuity between the care given during pregnancy and the care rendered during labor and birth. Midwives in hospitals work in shifts and will not have previously met the women they care for in labor. In this organization, a birth plan might be expected to provide a compensation for the lack of continuity from pregnancy to childbirth.

In Göteborg, Sweden, there is only one large unit for maternity care, Sahlgrenska University (SU) Hospital. It consists of four delivery wards, situated in two different areas of Göteborg. The study was performed at SU/Östra, which has two delivery wards, one for women with normal pregnancy, and one "special delivery ward" for women who are at high obstetric risk or have obstetric complications. The women may choose between different delivery wards, but those with risk factors or with complications are referred to SU/Östra and the special delivery ward.

In the Göteborg area, there are 17 public antenatal care units and one private service. The private antenatal care unit is managed and owned by midwives but funded from the general health insurance program. A clinic for women who are at high obstetric risk or have obstetric complications is situated at the hospital, SU/Östra. The participants in this study were chosen from seven antenatal care units: five public, one private, and one for women either at high risk or with obstetric complications. Three antenatal care units are located in suburbs, one in the city center, and one in a mixed area. The private antenatal care unit is located in the city center. . . .

Hypotheses Challenged

Of the eligible women, 41 women were never invited due to the midwife's lack of time for giving informed consent, and 45 women declined participation. Altogether, 49 women were lost to follow-up secondary to transfer to another hospital. Two women had stillborn children. The responses of the first 271 women who followed this program were compared with the control group of 271 women. The respondent rate was 91% in the standard group and 98% in the intervention group. There was no difference in maternal characteristics between the control group and the study group. . . .

The hypothesis that the intervention, a questionnaire at the end of pregnancy followed by a birth plan, would improve women's experience of childbirth is rejected. When comparing results from the standard care group and the intervention group, women scored significantly lower in the intervention group in four of eight aspects of the relationship to the first

> ## The Birth Plan Trap
>
> A current fashion is the birth plan. Women write a birth plan with the intention of familiarizing themselves as well as protecting themselves from unnecessary interventions. . . .
>
> But there are flaws with this concept. First of all, there is no guarantee that her wishes will be honored. The birth plan is typically addressed to the doctor, who will not be one she will have to answer to in labor. . . .
>
> When a woman enters the hospital in labor, she must deal with the nurses and staff that happen to be on shift that day. These nurses do not know this woman, and are not aware of any agreement or discussion she has worked out ahead of time with the doctor.
>
> *Emily Jones, "The Birth Plan Trap,"*
> *www.truebirth.com, March 31, 2008*

midwife they encountered during childbirth: listening and paying attention to needs and desires, support, guiding (i.e., guidance from the midwife on the women's own terms), and respect. On the whole, the women gave high scores to questions about the relationship to the midwife, the physician, and the partner/other relative. More than 90% of the women in the standard care group scored high on statements concerning all aspects of their contact with the first midwife who cared for them during labor, except time and support to cope with pain.

There were no significant differences between the standard care group and the intervention group in the other categories: subsequent midwives who gave care during labor, physician, fear of childbirth, pain during childbirth, sense of control, concerns for the child, and the total experience.

The hypothesis that the intervention would be more positive for women with high socioeconomic status is also rejected. The main results indicate no difference related to socioeconomic status. However, the results indicate that some aspects of fear, pain, and concerns for the child were improved for some subgroups of women. Women with high socioeconomic status in the intervention group expressed less concern about the delivery as being difficult for the child. Both women with low socioeconomic status and primiparae [women giving birth for the first time] in the intervention group had a more positive experience of pain during labor. Multiparae [women who have given birth before] in the intervention group experienced less fear of giving birth and less fear of labor pain than the multipara women in the standard care group. . . .

The results indicate that the questionnaire at the end of pregnancy followed by development of a birth plan did not improve women's experience of childbirth; rather, some aspects of the relationship to the first midwife the woman encountered during childbirth (listening and paying attention to needs and desires, support, guiding, and respect) were experienced as less satisfactory after the intervention. The main results also found no difference related to socioeconomic status. However, some aspects of fear, pain, and concerns for the child were improved for some groups of women after the intervention, which should be further studied. Multiparae in the intervention group had less fear of giving birth and fear of labor pain in the intervention group than in the standard group. Primiparae and women with low socioeconomic status in the intervention group had a more positive experience of pain during labor. Women of high socioeconomic status in the intervention group scored lower concerning the delivery as being difficult for the child.

Birth Plans Are Not Always Necessary

According to [birth activist Sheila] Kitzinger, a primary objective for birth plans is to help to focus the relationship between the woman and her caregiver. When birth plans were introduced during the 1980s, several studies showed that communication difficulties were the main complaints among childbearing and birthing women. According to this study, women scored the relationship to the midwife very high, over 90% scoring 5 or 6 concerning the different aspects. This might explain why the intervention did not improve the relationship to the midwife because midwives are already very good at establishing caring relationships with the women. According to [researchers Yvonne] Bo Stock and [Inch], a birth plan may be unnecessary where hospital policies are flexible. This result must also be evaluated in relation to the context, a care system with a homogeneous group of midwives as caregivers. It's also notable that a birth plan is not an adequate compensation for the women for lack of continuity from pregnancy to childbirth.

Is it the uniform approach as such, with a birth plan for everybody, which results in a less positive experience in the intervention group? [Researchers Rhonda] Small et al. found that another intervention, debriefing after childbirth, is not associated with a reduction of depression 6 months after childbirth. The possibility that debriefing may contribute to emotional health problems for some women still cannot be excluded, according to Small et al. One explanation might be a secondary trauma, resulting from exposure to the experience during the debriefing session. Perhaps the birth plan provokes the woman to answer questions about the future childbirth, questions that she is not prepared to ponder. It is also possible that the birth plan may hinder the midwife from having a unique encounter with the women. If so, the birth plan becomes just another piece of paper to deal with for the midwife at the delivery unit, which directs her attention more to the birth plan than to the encounter with the woman.

Maybe the lower scoring for the first midwife the women encountered during childbirth is due to higher expectations after completing a birth plan. Studies that evaluate women's expectation and experiences of childbirth are few. [Scholars Josephine] Green et al. found that low expectations are related to a negative experience, but high expectations are not, per se, to be understood as detrimental to women. According to [Jo] Gibbins and [Ann M.] Thomson, a sense of being in control is most important in helping the woman to feel positive about the labor experience, also when it was different from their expectations. When birth plans were introduced, the intervention was expected to give the woman more control during childbirth. Control is associated with a positive experience of childbirth. Control is often understood as being able to control what is being done to one during childbirth but may also mean to be able to flow with the body. However, according to Green et al., involvement in decision-making may occasionally confuse the women and increase their anxiety levels. In the present study, the statements focusing on control concerned both control of what was being done and being able to flow with the body. There was no difference between the intervention group and the standard group concerning control during childbirth. That birth plans do not improve a woman's sense of control during childbirth has also been verified by [Heather M.] Whitford and [Edith M.] Hillan.

The hypothesis that women of higher socioeconomic status are in need of more control and that a birth plan would therefore be more positive for them is not supported by this study. This is also verified by [researchers David] Machin and [Mandie] Scamell who found that the divergences in priorities in different classes before childbirth decreased at the onset of labor, rendering delivery experiences more similar.

Some aspects of the experience of fear and pain were improved for some groups of women after intervention. According to Green, the pain caused by labor can provoke anxiety and fear. Fear of childbirth is related to negative childbirth experiences and posttraumatic stress disorder. In Sweden, as in other countries, women's demands for painless births via a caesarian section have increased. Whether a birth plan may improve a woman's experiences of pain and fear needs further investigation.

A questionnaire at the end of pregnancy, followed by a birth plan, was not effective in improving women's experience of childbirth. Instead, some aspects of the relationship with the first midwife the woman encounters during childbirth are experienced as less fulfilling after the intervention, even though the women generally scored high for their relationship with the midwife, the physician, and the partner/other relative. However, certain experiences of fear of childbirth, pain, and concerns for the child were improved for some groups of women. These aspects should be further studied. The findings highlight the complex nature of childbirth experiences. Furthermore, it stresses that new routines of care, such as birth plans, need to be evaluated before they are introduced as routine. In the context of this study, a care system with a homogeneous group of midwives as caregivers, a birth plan may form a barrier for the encounter between the midwife and the woman. More research is needed to evaluate if a birth plan may be useful in other contexts (e.g., with different caregivers and policies).

> "Most likely the overall health and welfare of the woman will be promoted by supporting her request [to have an elective cesarean section]."

Women Have the Right to Elective Cesareans

Mary E. Hannah

Mary Hannah is a researcher at the Centre for Research in Women's Health at the University of Toronto in Ontario, Canada. In the following viewpoint, she argues that if women feel strongly about planning a cesarean birth and they have been educated about the risks and benefits of the procedure, then health care providers should follow their requests. Given that cesarean deliveries have become much safer in recent years and that emergency cesarean sections are more risky than elective cesareans, there are few reasons to deny women the right to plan the birth of their children.

As you read, consider the following questions:

1. According to Hannah, how much more likely are mothers to die from an elective cesarean section compared to a vaginal birth?

Mary E. Hannah, "Planned Elective Cesarean Section: A Reasonable Choice for Some Women?" *Canadian Medical Association Journal*, vol. 170, March 2, 2004, pp. 813–814. Copyright © 2004 Canadian Medical Association. Reproduced by permission.

2. Why does having a cesarean delivery increase the risk of major bleeding in subsequent pregnancies, according to the author?

3. What does Hannah identify as the rate of emergency cesarean section for a term pregnancy with a baby in the breech position?

A growing number of women are requesting delivery by elective cesarean section without an accepted "medical indication," and physicians are uncertain how to respond. This trend is due in part to the general perception that cesarean delivery is much safer now than in the past and to the recognition that most studies looking at the risks of cesarean section may have been biased, as women with medical or obstetric problems were more likely to have been selected for an elective cesarean section. Thus, the occurrence of poor maternal or neonatal outcomes may have been due to the problem necessitating the cesarean delivery rather than to the procedure itself. The only way to avoid this selection bias is to conduct a trial in which women would be randomly assigned to undergo a planned cesarean section or a planned vaginal birth. When this was done in the international randomized Term Breech Trial involving 2088 women with a singleton fetus in breech presentation at term, the risk of perinatal or neonatal death or of serious neonatal morbidity was significantly lower in the planned cesarean group, with no significant increase in the risk of maternal death or serious maternal morbidity.

In response to the growing demand from women to have a planned elective cesarean section, the American College of Obstetricians and Gynecologists published a committee opinion that states

> If taken in a vacuum, the principle of patient autonomy would lend support to the permissibility of elective cesarean delivery in a normal pregnancy, after adequate informed consent. To ensure that the patient's consent is, in fact, in-

formed, the physician should explore the patient's concerns. . . . If the physician believes that cesarean delivery promotes the overall health and welfare of the woman and her fetus more than vaginal birth, he or she is ethically justified in performing a cesarean delivery. Similarly, if the physician believes that performing a cesarean delivery would be detrimental to the overall health and welfare of the woman and her fetus, he or she is ethically obliged to refrain from performing the surgery.

The Ethics Committee of the Society of Obstetricians and Gynecologists of Canada is also preparing a statement.

Risks and Benefits of Cesarean Delivery

What are the risks of cesarean delivery? The maternal mortality is higher than that associated with vaginal birth (5.9 for elective cesarean delivery v. 18.2 for emergency cesarean v. 2.1 for vaginal birth, per 100,000 completed pregnancies in the United Kingdom during 1994–1996). Cesarean section also requires a longer recovery time, and operative complications such as lacerations and bleeding may occur, at rates varying from 6% for elective cesarean to 15% for emergency cesarean. Having a cesarean delivery increases the risk of major bleeding in a subsequent pregnancy because of placenta previa (5.2 per 1000 live births) and placental abruption (11.5 per 1000 live births). Among term babies, the risk of neonatal respiratory distress necessitating oxygen therapy is higher if delivery is by cesarean (35.5 with a prelabour cesarean v. 12.2 with a cesarean during labor v. 5.3 with vaginal delivery, per 1000 live births). Also, a recent study has reported that the risk of unexplained stillbirth in a second pregnancy is somewhat increased if the first birth was by cesarean rather than by vaginal delivery (1.2 per 1000 v. 0.5 per 1000). Lastly, birth by cesarean is not generally considered "natural" or "normal."

What are the benefits of cesarean section? It may reduce the risk of urinary incontinence, which is a common postpar-

The Benefits of Elective Cesareans

Elective cesareans lessen or eradicate some of the risks associated with vaginal birth. Moms suffer less pain during delivery and don't have to deal with such problems as perineal tearing, urinary or fecal incontinence, or sexual dysfunction from pelvic floor damage. Instead of waiting anxiously for your contractions to kick in at any moment, you can rest assured since you know your due date.

The baby is at less risk for fetal distress or oxygen deprivation from long labor. Also, if your baby turns out to be larger than expected, he won't get injured coming through the birth canal or by forceps or other assisted-delivery equipment.

And, a pre-planned cesarean is safer than an emergency intervention one. "The safest c-section is a scheduled one," says Jacques Moritz MD, director of gynecology at St. Luke's/Roosevelt Hospital Center in New York City. "It's riskier if the woman has gone through labor and may already have complicating factors such as uterine infection or exhaustion as a result of prolonged labor, or if the head or shoulder is already engaged in the pelvis and then gets stuck there, making a c-section necessary but more risky."

Barbara Williams Cosentino,
"Elective Cesarean: Is It For You?"
September 2006, www.babycenter.com.

tum problem. In one study of primiparous women, 26% had urinary incontinence at 6 months postpartum, the rate being lowest with elective cesarean (5%), higher with cesarean during labour (12%), higher still following a spontaneous vaginal birth (22%) and highest following a vaginal forceps delivery (33%). Although not as common as urinary incontinence, fecal incontinence, affecting about 4% of women giving birth, is usually a serious problem, and the risk may be reduced by cesarean section. Other maternal benefits from cesarean delivery include avoidance of labour pain, alleviation of fear and anxiety related to labor or birth and reduced worry about the health of the baby. Also, some women may just prefer the convenience and control of being able to plan the precise timing of the birth. The baby may also benefit. The risk of an unexplained or unexpected stillbirth may be reduced by cesarean section, as may be the risk of complications of labor such as clinical chorioamnionitis, fetal heart rate abnormalities and cord prolapse. Lastly, labor and vaginal birth, complete with hospital stay, continuous electronic fetal heart rate monitoring, induction or augmentation of labor, epidural analgesia, forceps delivery, episiotomy and multiple caregivers, may also not be considered "natural" or "normal."

However, this issue involves more than a simple comparison of risks and benefits of cesarean and vaginal birth. Planning for a vaginal birth may result in an emergency cesarean section, which carries higher risks for the mother than if an elective cesarean had been undertaken. For a term pregnancy with a breech presentation, the risk of emergency cesarean is over 40%. If the baby is in a cephalic presentation, the risk of emergency cesarean may be less than 5% for a multiparous woman in spontaneous labor at 37 weeks' gestation, and as high as 35% for a primiparous woman who is having labour induced at 42 weeks' gestation. Other factors, such as maternal age, may also affect this risk. If the mother has a vaginal birth, it may have required a forceps delivery or resulted in tearing of the anal sphincter, or both, thus increasing the risks of urinary and fecal incontinence. Although pelvic floor muscle training may reduce the risk of postpartum incontinence, these exercises are not always prescribed by obstetric care providers.

Breech Births

The important question, therefore, is whether a planned cesarean delivery will be more beneficial than harmful to a woman and her baby compared with a planned vaginal birth. To answer this question for women with a singleton fetus in breech presentation at term, we undertook the international randomized controlled Term Breech Trial involving 2088 women. Most (90.4%) of the women randomly assigned to the planned cesarean group delivered by cesarean section; however, only 56.7% of the women randomly assigned to the planned vaginal birth group actually delivered vaginally, the others having complications that necessitated a cesarean section. Compared with planned vaginal birth, the policy of planned cesarean delivery reduced the risk of perinatal or neonatal death (0.3% v. 1.3%, $p < 0.01$) and the risk of perinatal or neonatal death or serious neonatal morbidity (1.6% v. 5.0%, $p < 0.0001$). There was one maternal death in the planned vaginal birth group. The risk of maternal death or serious short-term maternal morbidity was low among all women and not increased among women in the planned cesarean group (3.9% v. 3.2%, $p < 0.35$). However, when these results were included in a Cochrane review with two other small randomized trials, the risk of short-term maternal morbidity was significantly higher with a policy of planned cesarean section than with planned vaginal birth (relative risk 1.29, 95% confidence interval 1.03–1.61). On the basis of this information, the American College of Obstetricians and Gynecologists issued a committee opinion on breech delivery stating that "patients with a persistent breech presentation at term in a singleton gestation should undergo a planned cesarean delivery." And at 3 months after the birth, women in the planned cesarean group of the Term Breech Trial were less likely than women in the vaginal birth group to report urinary incontinence (4.5% v. 7.3%, $p < 0.02$).

Unfortunately, for women not having a breech birth, such as those pregnant with twins, women who have had a previous cesarean section, older women, those who are having their first baby, those with incontinence problems and women who are afraid of labour, we have little information on the true benefits and risks of planned elective cesarean section compared with planned vaginal birth. Randomized studies are underway involving women with twins and women who have had a previous low-segment cesarean section, but the findings will not be available for several years.

In the meantime, what should physicians do? Most women prefer to plan for a vaginal birth. However, if a woman without an accepted medical indication requests delivery by elective cesarean section and, after a thorough discussion about the risks and benefits, continues to perceive that the benefits to her and her child of a planned elective cesarean outweigh the risks, then most likely the overall health and welfare of the woman will be promoted by supporting her request.

> *"The trend toward elective C-section reveals problems with how we deal with childbirth and parenting in the U.S."*

Elective Cesareans Should Not Be Performed Routinely

Kathi Carlisle Fountain and Kristen Suthers

Kathi Carlisle Fountain is a librarian at California State University. Kristen Suthers is a program specialist at the National Women's Health Network, a women's advocacy organization. In the following viewpoint, they discuss the findings of a recent National Institutes of Health (NIH) conference on elective cesarean deliveries. They argue that due to lack of accurate data, the NIH's statement positively comparing the risks of elective cesarean sections to vaginal deliveries is misleading and could harm mothers and babies. Furthermore, they assert that childbirth practices in the United States should be examined before health care providers routinely perform cesarean sections upon maternal request.

As you read, consider the following questions:

1. According to Fountain and Suthers, what percentage of all U.S. births in 2004 were the result of cesarean delivery?

2. The resulting uterine scar tissue from cesarean delivery can cause what two issues in subsequent pregnancies, according to the authors?

3. According to the World Health Organization and "Healthy People 2010," what should be the percentage of all first deliveries carried about by cesarean section?

Recently, you may have read news articles stating that cesarean sections pose no extra risk to women who are giving birth, or that "it may be reasonable for many women to deliver by caesarean section even without a medical need." The truth, however, is much more complicated than these misleading sound bites suggest.

In late March [2006], the National Institutes of Health (NIH) convened a state-of-the-science conference entitled "Cesarean Delivery on Maternal Request" to explore the safety of elective cesarean section performed because the woman requested it rather than because it was medically necessary. (There are a range of situations in which U.S. providers typically judge vaginal birth's risks to be to be great enough to necessitate cesarean section—for example, when the baby is in distress or a breech position [feet first].) During the hearing's one and a half days, panelists reviewed the available scientific evidence and listened to comments and questions from advocates, scientists, and members of the health care community. It is clear, based on the evidence compiled by the panel, that very little research exists on the risks associated with cesarean sections that are chosen by the mother rather than being medically necessary.

On the conference's third day, the panel issued a report stating that there was "insufficient evidence to evaluate fully the benefits and risks" of cesarean sections requested by women. Despite the lack of evidence on this subject, the NIH panel concluded that the risks of natural birthing and medically unnecessary cesarean sections were essentially equal. The National Women's Health Network [NWHN] disagrees—we believe that there is not enough scientific evidence to support the panel's statement on the comparable risks of medically unnecessary cesarean sections and vaginal births.

Inadequate Data on "Maternal Requests"

The rise of elective cesarean sections was widely discussed at the NIH conference, including the fact that the number of cesarean sections is at an all-time high. In 2004, almost one-third (29%) of all U.S. births occurred as a cesarean section. Yet, it is virtually unknown how many of these cesareans are elective and requested by the mother. Some women choose to have a caesarean section that is not medically necessary because they fear complications associated with vaginal birth, worry that it will stretch the vaginal walls, or want to time delivery so that they will have help when they are back at home.

Hospital records and birth certificates do not clearly identify when a cesarean section is performed without medical reason at the mother's request. The only study to directly assess mothers' choices found that less than one percent of women chose to have a cesarean section that was not medically necessary. The incidence of medically unnecessary cesarean sections seems to be on the rise in the last five years, however, and recent media coverage of this issue has stimulated women's interest in whether this is a reasonable childbirth option.

Elective C-Section vs. Vaginal Delivery

Many women have heard negative stories about how vaginal birth can result in incontinence, sexual dysfunction, or pelvic organ prolapse. But, the NIH panel found only weak evidence

Making a Choice vs. Making an Informed Choice

Precepts of autonomy demand that women have the right to give their consent or refusal to any obstetric procedure, but there is a difference between making a choice and making an informed choice. It is unconscionable in any discussion of the comparative harms of elective cesarean versus planned vaginal birth to mislead women into thinking that cesarean surgery will not expose them and their babies to potentially severe consequences. It is equally unconscionable to give women the misimpression that the potential harms of cesarean surgery are counterbalanced by its protection of the pelvic floor. Beyond the first few months, there is at most a 4% excess chance of developing bothersome urinary incontinence with vaginal birth. . . . Indeed, ethics aside, it makes no logical sense to recommend prophylactic surgery for a condition for which only a small percentage of women may later want or require reparative surgery.

"Elective Cesarean Surgery Versus Planned Vaginal Birth:
What Are the Consequences?" Lamaze International,
www.lamaze.org.

connecting these problems to either vaginal or elective cesarean section birth. The best evidence on these birth consequences, labeled as "moderate" by the panel, indicates:

• Women's length of hospital stay is longer for those who have a cesarean section (whether elective or emergency), than for women who experience a vaginal delivery.

• Respiratory problems are much more common for babies delivered by cesarean section, especially those delivered before 39 weeks of gestation.

• Postpartum hemorrhage is more likely for women who attempt to deliver vaginally but have an emergency cesarean section.

Despite the lack of evidence on vaginal vs. cesarean births, we do know that cesareans carry risk for both women and their babies. Cesarean sections require an incision to be made into the uterus; in a subsequent pregnancy, the resulting scar tissue can cause the placenta to attach too deeply (a condition called "placenta accreta") or too low (called "placenta previa") in the uterus. The more children a woman delivers by cesarean section, the higher her risk for placenta abnormalities. Unfortunately, many hospitals and insurance policies increase women's risks by restricting them from delivering vaginally if they have had a cesarean before. As a result, a woman's first cesarean section can limit her to future cesarean sections, and higher risk of placenta problems. Therefore, the NIH panel recommended that women who intend to have more than one child should not have their first child by elective cesarean section.

We also know that pre-term cesarean delivery (e.g. delivery before 39 weeks of gestation) can inhibit the fetus' ability to transition to breathing air, which increases the risk that a newborn will spend time in the neonatal intensive care unit. For this reason, the NIH panel recommended that obs document lung maturity and gestational age before proceeding with an elective cesarean before 39 weeks.

Failure to Set Public Health Goals

The NIH panel explicitly rejected establishing optimal numeric goals for the prevalence of cesarean sections such as those set by other public health entities. (The World Health Organization and the U.S. government's "Healthy People 2010" standards both have a goal that no more than 15 percent of all first deliveries should occur by cesarean section.) Instead, the panel concluded that decisions on delivery modes should

165

be individualized and the conference statement asserts that: "optimal cesarean delivery rates will vary over time and across different populations according to individual and societal circumstances."

This stance might have far-reaching consequences for researchers who are attempting to track the prevalence, and analyze the safety, of different modes of delivery, as the elimination of numeric goals could reduce the likelihood that these data will be collected and made available. It may also make it harder for individual women who want to use such data to compare providers' track records so that they can select one who is more likely to support their decision to plan for a particular mode of delivery.

The NIH panel noted that most of the literature evaluating the risks of cesarean sections fails to distinguish between planned and emergency procedures, making it very difficult to state definitively the risks associated with elective cesareans. The panel concluded that more research is needed to determine the true risks and benefits of elective cesarean sections, and suggested exploring the feasibility of randomized trials.

The NWHN questions the practicality of such a randomized trial of birthing methods; a woman's preference for the type of delivery she wants is extremely likely to affect her birthing experience, and random assignment may skew the results because of participants' dissatisfaction with their assignment. Further, if the trial were restricted to women who have no preference between cesarean section and vaginal birth, it would bias the data, as women participating in such a study are likely to be atypical.

In theory, with good informed consent, elective surgery isn't unethical. But the trend toward elective c section reveals problems with how we deal with childbirth and parenting in the U.S. Women have valid reasons for being concerned about vaginal birth, but the NWHN believes we should address those concerns through research and training to improve women's birthing experiences, instead of turning to abdominal surgery as the solution.

Periodical Bibliography

The following articles have been selected to supplement the diverse views presented in this chapter.

Janet Bryanton, et al.	"Predictors of Women's Perceptions of the Childbirth Experience," *Journal of Obstetric, Gynecologic, and Neonatal Nursing*, vol. 37, no. 1, January/February 2008.
Marisa Cohen	"Have It Your Way," *Fit Pregnancy*, January 2007.
Maureen Connolly	"Owning Your C-Section," *Baby Talk*, June/July 2007.
Nancy Draznin	"Setting and Keeping Boundaries," *Special Delivery*, Summer 2007.
Christa Haynes	"Choices in Childbirth," *New Mexico Woman*, May 2006.
Bernadine Healy	"Birthing by Appointment," *U.S. News and World Report*, June 12, 2006.
Beth Howard	"Labor Day," *Baby Talk*, January 2008.
Deborah Kotz	"On Women: The Downside of C-Sections on Demand," *U.S. News & World Report*, January 23, 2008.
Shari Roan	"Planned C-Section Risks," *Fit Pregnancy*, September 2007.
Amy M. Romano and Judith A. Lothian	"Promoting, Protecting, and Supporting Normal Birth: A Look at the Evidence," *Journal of Obstetric, Gynecologic, and Neonatal Nursing*, vol. 37, no. 1, January/February 2008.
Marcy White	"Listening to Mothers II: Second National U.S. Survey of Women's Childbearing Experiences," *International Journal of Childbirth Education*, vol. 22, no. 1, March 2007.

OPPOSING
VIEWPOINTS®
SERIES

CHAPTER 4

Who Should Assist and Be Present During Childbirth?

Chapter Preface

In recent decades, it has become increasingly common for fathers to assist and participate in the delivery of their children. At the same time, a trend of men bestowing lavish postnatal gifts on the mothers of their children has arisen in the United States and elsewhere. The tradition seems to have begun in Europe and Asia. English and Indian mothers were given extravagant gifts of diamonds and gold following the births of their babies. These so-called "push presents" often come in the form of valuable pieces of jewelry that can be passed down to future generations. In the last decade, this trend has spread to the United States, where the gifts have taken different forms, including "babymoons"—postpartum romantic getaways—and all-day spa treatments. A recent survey of more than 30,000 women conducted by BabyCenter-.com revealed that more than 38 percent of new mothers received some type of "baby bauble" after the birth of their children. In fact, this trend has become so popular that companies like Tiffany's and Austin and Warburton have started marketing jewelry specifically designed for this joyous occasion. While many new mothers appreciate, and even expect, such a reward, opponents of bequeathing push presents question the message it sends.

The reasons given for postnatal gift giving are numerous. A woman labors for hours—even days—to give birth to a child that she has carried for more than nine months. A post-birth gift allows partners to honor mothers' hard work, to commemorate the event, and to demonstrate their love and appreciation for the mothers and their newborn children. According to Linda Murray, the executive editor of BabyCenter-.com, "It's more and more an expectation of moms these days that they deserve something for bearing the burden for nine months, getting sick, ruining their body." *New York Times* reporter Thomas Vinci Guerra cites a different motivation for giving push presents: "A more likely explanation is that men are now simply more aware of and sympathetic to the plight of their pregnant partners, given their increasing tendency to attend childbirth classes and help in the actual delivery."

Nonetheless, not all couples agree with these postpartum gifts. Some people are concerned that this trend commercializes the birth experience and those fathers might give push presents only because of peer pressure. Furthermore, according to village correspondent Kate Schweitzer, "Many budget-conscious couples believe that spending thousands of dollars on something other than their new baby is irresponsible, especially when new expenses, such as education, develop." In addition, Strollerderby blogger Rachel Brownell wonders if this trend of gift giving will result in a type of warped value being assigned to different birth experiences. She asks, "Is thirty hours of labor worth more than only twenty? If the labor is all-natural is that more valuable than one requiring an epidural or C-section? What about birthing multiples?"

Perhaps Vinci Guerra is right in that as more fathers get involved in the births of their children, the more appreciative they become of their partners' hard work in bringing a new life into the world. While the presence of fathers in the delivery room has become commonplace, some still debate whether the father's participation is a help or a hindrance. The authors in this chapter discuss the value of the father's presence as well as that of other helpers in the delivery room, revealing many facets of a complex question.

> "[Doulas] provide a link between doctors—who are too busy, usually, to spend much time with expectant moms—and the couple."

Doulas Can Be Helpful During Childbirth

Kristen Davenport

In the following viewpoint, Kristen Davenport explains how having a doula can be helpful during childbirth, not only for a mother, but for everyone in the family. A doula is even affordable—some hospitals offer doulas on a sliding scale and insurance companies like doulas because they reduce the cost of having a baby. Doulas have been proven to reduce the rate of cesarean sections by half and the request for epidurals by 60 percent. While doulas have less medical training than midwives, they provide support before, after, and during the birth. Doulas help by answering questions mothers are too embarrassed to ask their doctors, by helping fathers to become better birth coaches, and by explaining events that are taking place. In addition, doulas have a reassuring effect by their constant presence and ability to anticipate the needs of laboring women.

Kristen Davenport, "Mothering the Mothers," *The Santa Fe New Mexican* (Santa Fe, NM), April 28, 2000. Reproduced by permission.

As you read, consider the following questions:

1. How does the author describe the role of a doula?

2. What are some of the effects the presence of a doula has been proven to have on labor?

3. How can using a doula reduce the costs of having a baby?

Doulas pay extra attention to mothers, answer jittery parents' questions—and can even reduce the cost of having a baby.

When Kim Henning went into labor in the middle of the night, about to give birth to Julia (who, we know in retrospect, looks like her grandpa), Karen Woods was quite happy to run over and make smoothies for the expectant family.

Woods, a longtime Santa Fe doula, arrived with the sunrise at the Santa Fe home of Kim and her husband, Steve Brock, who had their first child March 30. She put Kim in the bathtub before getting out the blender to make smoothies so the couple would have some food in their bellies before going to the hospital.

Hopefully, with the new doula program at St. Vincent Hospital, many soon-to-be parents will have such bath-side service.

Doulas—"Mothering the Mother"

Doula is a Greek word meaning "mothering the mother" or "mother's helper." Doulas are women with less actual medical training than midwives who provide support—and advice, and funny stories, and sometimes smoothies—to the mother and the family before and after the birth.

St. Vincent Hospital has a program beginning this month [April 2000] that provides doulas on a sliding scale to all mothers who plan to have babies at the hospital. They hope to have doulas for teen mothers and low-income moms who might not typically decide to have that kind of support.

Generally, in Santa Fe, doulas charge about $450. St. Vincent will have half a dozen doulas on staff; clients who can pay full price and perhaps some grant money will make up for new moms who can't afford the full cost.

They provide a link between doctors—who are too busy, usually, to spend much time with expectant moms—and the couple.

"Doctors have four to seven minutes to see the patient (who is in labor)," Woods said. "They don't have time for emotional support."

So doulas hold hands, coach through breathing and contractions, and answer weird and sometimes awkward questions.

And they share the joy when Julia is born and her dad notices that she has her grandfather's features.

"She looks like my dad," Steve Brock said the morning after Julia was born.

"She looks like you," Woods said to Brock. "She looks even more like you today."

Although the doula is largely there for the mother, Woods said she also tries to work with the fathers.

"I usually give the baby a bath with the father afterwards," said Woods, who also teaches St. Vincent's prenatal class.

Doulas Reduce Cost and Stress of Having a Baby

Here's something unusual—even insurance companies like doulas (many plans will pay for them) because they reduce the cost of having a baby.

Doulas have been proven to reduce the rate of cesarean sections by half and the requests for epidurals (a shot into the back to relieve pain) by 60 percent. Even labor is shorter—studies show the length of labor is reduced by about 25 percent when a doula is there to mother the mother. Other pain drugs used are reduced by about 30 percent.

Most doulas are not, however, adamantly opposed to common drugs given during childbirth; instead, they ask a couple to write a birth plan before labor starts outlining their wishes in all those areas. Epidural? Episiotomy? Would the couple like to be left alone with the baby after the birth? What if something goes wrong?

"We were so calm for our birth," Kim Henning said. "But we were calm because we knew Karen was coming and checking on us. We weren't alone."

In the weeks and months leading up to the birth, a doula meets with the expectant couple to talk about those issues and answer jittery parents' questions.

How can you tell what's real labor and what's just the unborn child fidgeting before it's really time? What if my water breaks in the store? What is meconium, anyway? (Answer to that last one: Unless you're pregnant, you probably don't want to know. . . .)

Santa Fe parents-to-be Wendy and Tom O'Neil met with Woods several times before their child was born in January.

Beforehand, the O'Neils didn't know what gender their baby was. Woods guessed it was a girl—"sometimes you just get a hit," she said. "It seems like Tom would have a girl."

Thus proving doulas aren't infallible. Charlie, very much a little baby boy, was born Jan. 27.

Taking Care of the Details

But Woods also helped the couple with dozens of other things at meetings in her office at the hospital and a visit to their home. Much of it was chatting, getting to know each other so when labor began, the three would be comfortable together in the delivery room.

"The (unborn) baby loves concerts," Wendy said, adding that it seemed to dance in her belly. "We took it to the Paramount (dance club) on Halloween."

(Wendy was dressed, by the way, as Humpty Dumpty.)

175

"Oh, you should take it to the African drumming on Saturday," Woods responded. "Just go and sit."

But some of it is serious. Wendy asked how she'd know when to call Woods to come to the hospital.

"You'll know," Woods said. "Trust me."

But she also explained what happens when the cervix starts to dilate—and told Wendy how to perform her own anatomy-check to see what's going on.

The couple wanted to know what happens if the baby is late and has meconium—feces from the placental fluid—on it when born.

Wendy was a bit worried about the pain, not knowing what to expect.

"I'd like to go as long as possible (without drugs)," Wendy said. "But I've never been through it. I just don't know."

"I would be concerned if you weren't that open," Woods said. "You have to keep your options open."

Tom was nervous, worried about the role of the father in the labor and delivery rooms.

"My husband was the same way," Woods said. "He said the hardest part was watching me in pain."

Woods, who has three children of her own, became a doula after her best female friend attended her first child's birth.

"I was just so glad there was another woman there (while I was in labor)," she said. "My husband left and when he'd come back I would feel like I had to be strong again. I could fall apart with her, for just a second."

After the Birth

Doulas also are usually present after the birth. For Wendy and Tom O'Neil, Woods went out to their house in Rowe the day after they went home because Wendy was having trouble breast feeding. For Henning and Brock, she was at the hospital—watching Julia sleep. And sleep. And sleep.

"They wake up after about three days," Woods said.

It's that kind of information that helps make sense out of something so unknown as a first child, Henning said.

"I felt like people were concerned, instead of feeling like I was just a machine producing a baby," she said.

And because St. Vincent has doulas on staff, doctors who deliver babies will know them, and hopefully trust them. The doula will be able to call ahead to the hospital when a woman goes into labor so the couple doesn't have to go through the red-tape rigmarole of enrolling when they arrive at the hospital.

"She (Woods) had already called the hospital and told them we were coming," so they weren't stopped at the door, said Henning, who only labored at the hospital for about three hours before her baby was born.

"Yep, I flashed my badge," Woods said. "I'm the doula lama."

| "I wasn't prepared for having to defend myself from the women that I had expected to help me feel empowered."

Doulas Can Be Too Controlling During Childbirth

Lucy Freeman

Lucy Freeman is a writer who focuses on women's issues. In the following viewpoint, she describes her experiences with pregnancy and childbirth support personnel and services in the United Kingdom. In particular, she argues that doulas might not be a good choice for all women because they can be aggressive, controlling, and misinformed. She draws on the commendations of Sue Macdonald of the Royal College of Midwives, who advises that doulas should be chosen carefully for the best birth experience.

As you read, consider the following questions:

1. In Freeman's opinion, why have doulas become more popular with women in the United Kingdom in recent years?

2. According to the author, why did a support group tell her not to keep infant formula in her house?

3. According to Sue Macdonald, what type of support
   should doulas provide to expectant mothers?

I'd always considered myself to be fairly assertive, and even more so during pregnancy. I felt ready to tackle any unwanted medical interventions during labor, and to make sure that I got the birth that I wanted, within reason. But I wasn't prepared for having to defend myself from the women that I had expected to help me feel empowered and have the natural birth I had always wanted: the complementary practitioners, doulas (female birthing partners), and birth support groups.

This was my second pregnancy and I was keen to experience a "proper" delivery (I'd had a caesarean with my first baby, as she was breech). A friend recommended an antenatal yoga class. At my first session, I realized that this wasn't so much a yoga class as a lesson in how to fight the [United Kingdom's free National Health Service] NHS. Women in the final stages of pregnancy were being advised not to attend their weekly meetings with their consultants as there was no need, and we were told the minutiae of our legal rights relating to home births, how much we could "demand" (rather than "request"), and how we could feel free to ignore our midwives' advice as they were "just trying to make things easier for themselves".

My yoga teacher asked me to relate my labor history. I was explaining that I had a C-section with my first baby when she interrupted to say triumphantly: "Let me guess, they've insisted that you have a caesarean this time." I pointed out gently that, on the contrary, "they" had said that I could have a normal delivery, and that I could have a home birth if I wanted.

I attended a second class, with misgivings. This time a nervous woman was explaining that she would be going to hospital the following week, and that she felt more comfortable with the thought of being in hospital than delivering the

Double Discord

There are no national statistics on the phenomenon, and few women readily admit to doula discord. But according to a 2006 study of women who used doulas in Alabama, 44 percent of women described the relationship between their hospital nurses and doulas as hostile, resentful and confrontational.

At Reston Hospital Center in northern Virginia, disputes became so common that in 2005, the hospital banned doulas. "From a nursing standpoint, too many crossed a line and interfered with my job," said Sarah Baxter, a registered nurse and director of labor and delivery at Reston.

Pamela Paul, "And the Doula Makes Four,"
The New York Times, *March 2, 2008.*

baby at home. There was a sharp intake of breath around the room and the teacher turned to her and said: "Why are you making it easier for them? Stand up for yourself." My friend in the class said cheerfully that when she had her first baby she wouldn't have noticed "whether I was delivering it in my bathroom or Piccadilly Circus as I just wasn't aware of my surroundings." The yoga teacher looked horrified and returned to the nervous woman, instructing her crisply: "You are *not* to have an epidural just because you're in hospital". I found her dogmatism so irritating that I didn't attend another class.

Finding No Reassurance

A session with a doula was no more comforting. Doulas have become increasingly popular in recent years as overstretched midwives have found it difficult to spend time supporting women in the run-up to birth. My doula began her class for mums-to-be by telling us that our birthing plans were considered to be legal documents. She had suggested to a woman whose labour she had attended recently that she stipulate that the midwife could enter the labour room "only after knocking and waiting to be admitted". She also suggested that one of my first acts should be to write to the chief executive of the hospital where I intended to have my baby and inform him or her that I had "no intention of allowing my labor to be placed in jeopardy because of the staff shortages at your hospital, and I, therefore, insist on a home birth being attended by one midwife throughout the entire labour". As labor can go on for three days, this was not a reassuring prospect.

I had thought that doulas did not have formal medical knowledge, nor did they need any, as their role was to be a support and mother-figure. Mine seemed to be militant in her attitude towards non-intervention and keen to tell me of many incidences in which she had urged mothers to act against the medical advice of their midwives. She was hostile in the extreme to the NHS. As the care I had received thus far from the NHS midwifery team had been warm, friendly and proactive I hurriedly dropped the doula, too.

As I moved house halfway through my pregnancy, I experienced two different National Childbirth Trust (NCT) groups [which offers free support for parents during pregnancy, childbirth, and early parenthood]. One fulfilled the charity's stated mission: it was supportive, helpful, and relaxed. The other was authoritarian, instructing us not to have formula milk in the house as it might seduce us away from breast-feeding. I had been in the unhappy position with my first child of suffering acute mastitis on a weekend and was unable to breast-feed my screaming daughter. Luckily my partner had bought some formula, "just in case".

The militancy extended to natural births, and a friend of mine confided that she had been too ashamed to attend her post-natal support meetings with her local NCT group because she had "given in" and had an epidural.

I know that this militant attitude does not apply to all those who advocate natural birth. Many women feel that complementary practitioners, doulas and NCT groups have given them a sense of control that they would not otherwise have had, but I never expected that they would make me feel the opposite.

As it turned out, I did have a caesarean as my baby son was huge and two weeks overdue, something I am sure the doula and the yoga teacher would have had a great deal to say about. My friendly and sympathetic NHS consultant simply said "good choice", and smiled.

Happy Birth Days

When looking for non-medical help, Sue Macdonald, the education and research midwife at the Royal College of Midwives, suggests the following:

> All women should have care and support from a registered midwife; doulas provide social, not medical, support.
>
> If you're taking advice from someone else as well as your midwife, tell your midwife from the outset who you are talking to, whether they will be attending the birth and in what capacity.
>
> Ask your midwife to recommend an ante-natal class and a fitness class if you're interested.
>
> Training can vary enormously—use a registered doula. . . .
>
> If you want a relaxed labor you need to be surrounded by relaxed and positive people.
>
> Don't assume that the NHS is rigid. It has a wide range of labour options.

> "A midwife makes sense for any woman who has a low-risk pregnancy, doesn't have serious health problems, and wants to be more in charge of her labor and delivery."

Midwives Are a Good Choice for Some Women

Jon Marshall

Jon Marshall is a writer and journalism lecturer at Northeastern University. In the following viewpoint, he debunks some of the common myths about midwives. In addition, he argues that women with uncomplicated pregnancies should consider hiring midwives because they can offer more personalized support than most other health care providers can. He offers tips for finding a qualified midwife and discusses the possibilities for insurance coverage of midwife services.

As you read, consider the following questions:

1. On average, how many babies do midwives currently deliver annually, according to Jon Marshall?
2. According to the American College of Nurse-Midwives, what percentage of midwives practice in hospitals?

3. What does Marshall cite as the national cesarean rate for midwives?

When Joanie Holmes, of Hooper, Utah, became pregnant, she started seeing an ob-gyn who'd been recommended by a friend. "But after two appointments, I switched to a midwife whom my mom had suggested," she says. "To my doctor, I was 'just another delivery,' but the midwife really took the time to get to know me and understand how I wanted to give birth."

While physician-attended births are still the norm in the United States, the number of babies delivered by midwives is on the rise. Today, midwives deliver more than 310,000 babies—7 percent of all births. That number has more than doubled since 1990.

Though the image of midwives is changing, lots of people still think of them as untrained "coaches" who deliver babies at home or who insist that you give birth without drugs. If that's been your impression, read on for four things you didn't know about midwives—and why you may want to consider finding one for your next pregnancy.

Debunking Midwife Myths

1. Midwives have gone mainstream. Unlike doulas or birthing assistants, whose main job is to comfort a woman during labor, most midwives are medical professionals with varying amounts of formal training.

"When my friends found out I had a midwife, most of them assumed I was giving birth at home," says Jennifer Martin, of Eldridge, Iowa. "But my son, Jonathan, was born in a hospital." In fact, 97 percent of midwives practice in hospitals, according to the American College of Nurse-Midwives. Only about 2 percent deliver in birthing centers, and 1 percent in homes. Certified nurse-midwives can also administer labor-inducing drugs and epidurals.

2. Using a midwife is just as safe as using a doctor. Studies show that moms who use midwives have increased access to prenatal care, lower rates of cesarean births and obstetric interventions, and babies with higher birth weights. In addition, even homebirths for low-risk pregnancies using certified professional midwives are just as safe as low-risk hospital births, according to a study published in 2005 in the *British Medical Journal*. In Japan, Sweden, and the Netherlands, where midwives deliver almost all babies, infant mortality rates are much lower than in the U.S., according to the National Center for Health Statistics.

3. Midwives focus on physical and emotional support. A midwife makes sense for any woman who has a low-risk pregnancy, doesn't have serious health problems, and wants to be more in charge of her labor and delivery. Midwife literally means "with woman," and that's her greatest strength—a nurturing, woman-centered approach. "My midwife listened to me and respected my input," says Eireann Kiley of North Adams, Massachusetts. "She really took the time to get to know me and my husband." Midwives are likely to spend more time with you than most doctors and offer both emotional and physical support during prenatal visits, labor, delivery, and the postpartum period. "Midwives are especially good at helping new moms with breastfeeding, handling anxieties, and improving nutrition," says David Katz, MD, director of the Yale-Griffin Prevention Research Center, in Derby, Connecticut.

4. Midwives favor less invasive birth practices. Though midwives will help administer pain medication if a mom wants it, they tend to favor natural methods to ease the pain of labor and delivery. For example, they might give a mom a deep massage or encourage her to use an exercise ball to feel more comfortable, a warm compress to help the area stretch naturally and avoid tearing, or even a Jacuzzi to relax. These techniques can prevent episiotomies (the cutting of tissue to widen the birth canal) and help nature take its course, says Shafia

---

Intervention in Childbirth

The Midwives Alliance of North America's position is that childbirth is a normal physiological process as well as a social event in the life of a woman and her family. . . .

In keeping with this position, the midwife will:

promote childbirth practices, which enhance the normal physiological process;

promote the allocation of resources towards measures which support the basic needs of women and their babies as a priority, such as improved nutrition and social support during pregnancy;

continuously evaluate intervention and the use of technology in midwifery practice and take measures to avoid unnecessary interference; and

provide information to women and their families, which enhances the understanding of birth as a normal life process and enables them to make informed decisions.

"Intervention in Childbirth,"
Midwives Alliance of North America, 2008, www.mana.org.

Monroe, founder of the International Center for Traditional Childbearing, in Portland, Oregon. In fact, recent national studies show that the cesarean-section rate for midwives is 11.6 percent, one third that of the national rate. Midwives also have more successful VBAC (vaginal birth after cesarean) rates than the national averages. All this means that women who choose midwives are more likely to have a natural vaginal birth and to recuperate faster.

Is She Qualified?

CNMs (certified nurse-midwives) typically deliver in hospitals and birthing centers. These are registered nurses with advanced training in obstetrics and gynecology as well as specialized midwifery training; they've passed a certification exam and are licensed to practice in all 50 states. Many CNMs are employed by a hospital or work with a physician for consultation as needed. In most states, they can prescribe medication.

CM (certified midwife) is another credential from the American College of Nurse-Midwives. It doesn't require a nursing degree but, aside from that, certification is the same as that for a CNM.

CPMs (certified professional midwives) are accredited through exams by the North American Registry of Midwives, and their legal status varies according to state. They deliver babies mostly in homes or birthing centers.

"Lay" midwives—caregivers who've had only informal training—deliver babies without being certified by any national organization. Some states have very strict standards; others don't regulate midwives at all. . . .

How to Find a Good Midwife

- Ask your doctor, friends, relatives, other moms, or childbirth teacher for suggestions.

- Check with your local hospital to find out which midwives, if any, deliver babies there. Make sure you check references and credentials before making a final decision.

- The American College of Nurse-Midwives has about 6,200 practicing members. Visit midwife.org to find a registered nurse-midwife near you.

- The Midwives Alliance of North America (mana.org) is a national organization that represents midwives. Go to its Web site or to midwifeinfo.com for lists of mid-wives, including those who do homebirths.

Thirty-three states mandate that insurance companies in every state reimburse the cost of hiring a nurse-midwife, and most of the big health-insurance companies cover midwife services in every state. Check with your insurer to find out what your carrier allows.

> *"Fathers today . . . are expected to reinforce what has been taught in childbirth education, act as advocates for the mother, and fill gaps in care."*

Fathers Should Be Present During Childbirth

Fatherhood Institute

The Fatherhood Institute is a fathers' rights advocacy group based in the United Kingdom. In the following viewpoint, they argue that there are many benefits of fathers being present at the birth of their children. Not only do fathers help mothers-to-be feel greater comfort and satisfaction with their labor and delivery, but well-prepared fathers can also make up for inattentive medical personnel. Furthermore, according to the Institute, fathers who participate in the birth of their children are much more likely to be involved in their lives as they grow up.

As you read, consider the following questions:

1. According to the Fatherhood Institute, what percentage of fathers who live with their partners attend the births of their children?

2. How much more often are fathers likely to touch their partners during labor than other caregivers, according to the author?

3. In the author's opinion, a woman's fear of vaginal delivery is strongly associated with what factor?

Fifty years ago, very few fathers attended their children's births. Today 93% of fathers who live with their partners do so, as do 45% of those who live separately. NHS [United Kingdom's National Health Service] data shows even higher figures: 98% of fathers attending the birth, 48% attending antenatal/parenting classes, 85% at least one prenatal appointment with a midwife, and 86% at least one ultrasound scan.

[Murray] Enkin et al. note that fathers today have an expanded role in the birth process: they are expected to reinforce what has been taught in childbirth education, act as advocates for the mother, and fill gaps in care.

Benefits of the Father's Presence

With only a very few fathers not present (and those being almost exclusively men who are not in a close relationship with the baby's mother), it is difficult to make valid comparisons between the impact of fathers' presence in, or absence from, the labor room. However, being present allows many fathers to offer quality support—and this is clearly beneficial.

Earlier studies found that women whose husbands were present and supportive during labor were less distressed.

More recently, [researchers] found that laboring women benefit when they feel 'in control' of the birth process—and that a key component in this is experiencing support from their partner during the birth.

Support during delivery provided by a 'close support person' (who can be, and often is, the baby's father) creates a more positive childbirth experience for the mother, with a shorter duration of delivery and less pain experienced.

Enkin et al. report that when labor partners (including fathers) know a lot about pain control, women have shorter labors and are less likely to have epidurals. This support has also been found to be conducive to a more positive attitude by the mother towards motherhood.

Recent research from China differentiated between types of support, noting that level of perceived partner-provided emotional support did not result in positive maternal outcomes, while the perceived level of practical support did, including a strong correlation between duration of partners' presence during labor and women's ratings of perceived practical support by their partners.

However, a stressed birth partner can be counterproductive: stress, like fear, can contaminate—and maternal stress can slow down labour. Fathers' stress levels are often very high at key points during the birthing process. [Ed] Keogh et al. found caesarian mothers' post-operative pain strongly linked to their fear-experiences during labor, and these were mediated by the level of their birth partner's fear.

Benefits of Well-Prepared Fathers

Fathers who have been prepared well to participate productively in the labour process tend to be more active participants, and their partners' birth-experiences tend to be better.

Even where fathers have been only minimally prepared, studies repeatedly show high levels of satisfaction postpartum for both mothers and fathers in sharing the experience of labor and birth.

Fathers' presence has been shown to help compensate for poor quality obstetric services. [Researchers] found fathers five times more likely to touch their partner during labor and delivery than other support figures; and the women rated the fathers' presence more helpful than that of the nurses.

[Helen] Spiby et al. found laboring women generally disappointed by the level of midwife involvement while their partner's involvement much more nearly met their expectations—a personal experience also reported by [Julia] Llewellyn Smith.

Obstetricians greatly underestimate the psychological boost fathers give to their partners during delivery—as well as the practical support the men provide during labor, and afterwards.

Claims about long term negative effects of fathers' attending the birth have been made, particularly on the couple's sexual relationship but not substantiated through serious research. One well designed study showed that while negative perceptions of the birth-experience were correlated with depressive symptoms in fathers at six weeks postpartum, their effect was removed once pre-existing depressive symptoms were controlled for.

Greater Involvement Later

Birth attendance by fathers is not correlated with higher levels of involvement in, say, nappy [diaper] changing; however birth attendance followed by extensive postpartum father-infant interaction in the hospital may stimulate such behavior.

[Trevena] Moore & [Milton] Kotelchuck found a significant correlation between fathers' attendance at the birth and subsequent involvement in monitoring infant health by participating in 'well child visits'.

[Kathleen] Kiernan compared the behavior of non-resident fathers who had signed their baby's birth certificate with fathers who had not signed the birth certificate but had been present at their baby's birth. She found that though roughly equal numbers of both groups later moved in with their baby's mother, all other measures of involvement, except the payment of child support, were higher among the men who had attended the birth. Noting the many studies that have recorded the powerful impact on fathers of witnessing the births of their children, Kiernan comments: 'our evidence suggests that this attachment exemplified through presence at the birth carries through into infancy even among non-resident fathers'.

Relationship Quality Is Key

A woman's fear of vaginal delivery is strongly associated with her dissatisfaction with the couple relationship.

[Marja-Terttu] Tarkka found that one of three predictors of a young mother's positive childbirth experience was her perception of a positive attitude toward the pregnancy by the baby's father.

The best predictor of each parent's adjustment to parenthood is the quality of the relationship between them.

Women who enjoy the full support of their partners are more closely bonded to their children, and more responsive and sensitive to their needs.

The quality of mothering provided to an infant has been linked with support the mother receives from her partner; and the quality of the relationship between the parents has been shown to predict how both mother and father nurture and respond to their children's needs.

This is also true for teenage mothers: a young mother's perception of support from her baby's father correlates with a range of attachment behaviours by her.

Firstborns with highly involved fathers are more positive and accepting towards their second-born sibling.

Frequent care-taking of a firstborn by the father is associated with large increase in the firstborn's positive behaviours toward the mother, after the birth of a second sibling.   .

> *"Even men don't even seem convinced that they have a role to play in witnessing childbirth."*

Fathers Should Not Be Present During Childbirth

Sandra Dick

In the following viewpoint, Sandra Dick, a writer from Scotland, argues that men should think carefully about whether or not they want to attend the births of their children. Drawing on personal experience and recent studies, she asserts that fathers-to-be generally make laboring mothers more anxious and are often inattentive to their needs. She also notes that women continue to accept the idea of a perfect birth put forward by women's magazines, which encourages them to ask their partners to be with them in the delivery room. Unfortunately, Dick states, expectant fathers are not always up to the challenge.

As you read, consider the following questions:

1. According to one survey, what percentage of women believe that the fathers of their unborn children should not be in the delivery room?

2. Fifty years ago, what percentage of fathers attended the births of their children, as reported by the author?

3. According to a survey conducted by the Royal College of Midwives, how many fathers reported feeling "fairly useless" during their partner's labor and delivery?

It was the moment my husband mentioned to the midwife how dreadfully painful his triple heart bypass operation had been, that really did it.

Lying there in the throes of a drug-free 14-hour labor, wracked with excruciating pain, being slowly and tortuously ripped apart by the alien life form inside me and in no mood for pleasant chit-chat about how having a baby is probably a breeze compared with open heart surgery, I finally snapped.

Of course, several years later I can't remember the exact phrase I bellowed at my startled husband, although I'm pretty sure it was a slightly more colorful version of "shut up or get out, you berk".

Didn't he know that I was having a baby, for goodness sake? And at that precise moment in time, no-one on this planet could possibly be enduring more pain than me—and that included triple heart bleeding bypass patients.

Sadly, worse was to come.

Being a scientist who rather fancies himself as a bit of an amateur medic, my other half took just a bit too much interest in what kind of needle the midwife had chosen to perform her rather unpleasant embroidery on my nether regions, embarked on a long discussion on various stitches he had endured—none in quite as personal a place as mine though, so I beat him on that count—and then, to top it all, discovered they had a mutual acquaintance who had to be discussed at length while I lay back, legs akimbo, ignored.

It was probably my own fault for allowing him anywhere near the delivery room. For the truth is that a fair number of women—38 percent according to one survey—believe the best, and possibly safest, place for their man is on the other side of the labor ward.

Pressure to Attend the Birth

No doubt Mrs. David Cameron would disagree. Her husband, the Conservative leader and self-appointed father of the year [of Great Britain], has just suggested that men should follow him into the inner sanctum of the midwife's lair, to observe the "magic moment"—that's his words, not his wife's—of childbirth, to mop the little lady's sweaty brow.

Indeed, during a speech to the National Family and Parenting Institute, he pontificated: "Some relationship experts describe the moment of childbirth as the magic moment which can either play a key part in bonding a couple and increasing parental responsibility, or is a missed opportunity which leaves a couple drifting further apart and on a downward spiral."

Goodness. Well, if men ever felt under pressure to witness for themselves the gruesome and bloody spectacle of childbirth, they most certainly will now. And, likewise, if their partner ever felt they would rather keep all that messy business between her and the professionals, then, quite frankly, she's had her chips.

Unlike 50 years ago, when barely five per cent of men attended the birth of their child. Back then, men's job was to quite rightly disappear for a few hours to allow the women to get on with it. They then were expected to reappear within seconds of the birth with a big bunch of flowers.

Now it is estimated that around 96 percent of dads-to-be are in those delivery rooms—but just how many are there through choice, and how many because they are now expected to be there? Chances are, if they are there because they feel they've got to, then they'll be about as useful as a pair of size 5 Pampers pull-ups on a newborn's bum.

"He's a lot more supportive after his nap."

"He's More Supportive After His Nap," cartoon by Mike Baldwin. CartoonStock.com.

Not Always a "Magic Moment"

Some may well witness a relatively straight-forward, uncomplicated, entirely natural process. They might even get through the event without incurring the wrath of their hormonally wracked partner. And perhaps everyone will leave the delivery room having experienced their own personal "magic moment".

Others, sadly, will witness childbirth in all its spectacular gore—the kind of Technicolor horror that the pregnancy magazines skim over, the emergency caesarian, the forceps delivery, the cord around their baby's neck . . . and much, much worse.

Add to that the research which suggests that nervous men probably do more damage than good in the delivery suite: Bath University looked at caesarian births, and found that anxious men passed on their fears to their partners who, in turn, spoke of experiencing more pain afterwards. Therefore, I wonder, does that sound like a particularly good bonding experience.

Even men don't even seem that convinced that they have a role to play in witnessing childbirth. Four in ten fathers, according to a recent Royal College of Midwives survey, admit they feel "fairly useless" during the birth—hence the annoying drivel they begin to speak just as their partner's pain reaches an agonizing crescendo.

Still, we women are our own worst enemies. We buy into the baby magazine's idea of childbirth. We consume soothing words of wisdom about the vital role our partner can play: how he can be on hand to switch on our favourite CD at the right moment, to rummage in our bag for an energy bar and how he will smother us with love and affection while we both coo at our newborn.

Ladies, be warned. The reality is that he's probably switched your James Blunt CD for his Black Sabbath one, he'll have eaten the muesli bar and would rather hug the barman at his local during a post-natal booze-up.

Still, I suppose my husband's attendance during the birth of our first son six years ago couldn't have been that bad. Three years later, he was back by my side again. And yes, actually, he was just as annoying the second time around as he was the first time.

| "Grandparents can be great attendants at your birth if they are welcome and prepared."

Grandmothers Can Be Helpful During Childbirth

Carolynn Bauer Zorn

Carolynn Bauer Zorn is the author of Attending Your Grandchild's Birth: A Guide for Grandparents. *In the following viewpoint, she argues that grandparents, especially the expectant mother's mother, can be great assets during childbirth if they are prepared for the experience. While she asserts that it is important the mothers-to-be have their wishes honored, grandparents can temporarily relieve fathers-to-be of their duties and can offer expectant mothers emotional and physical support during labor and delivery.*

As you read, consider the following questions:

1. What compromise does the author recommend for including grandmothers in the delivery process when the expectant mother does not have a close relationship with them?

2. What are some ways listed by the author that a grand-mother could prepare for being present in the delivery room?

3. In Zorn's opinion, how can grandparents offer support to the father-to-be during his wife's labor and delivery?

Did you invite your mother to be in the delivery room when you gave birth? Are you sorry you did? Are you planning to invite her but haven't been able to overcome your husband's objections? Has it been impossible for you and your husband to decide if you want any of your child's future grandparents to be at the birth?

Your Wishes Must Come First

Many expecting couples must deal with these questions as more and more hospitals allow guests in the birthing room and many of today's grandparents express a desire to be included at the birth.

If you don't have a close relationship with your mother or mother-in-law, then the obvious answer is to do what will make you most comfortable. This is your day, your body, and your birth experience. Your wishes should come first. If you and your husband disagree, then you must work it out before you head to the hospital. Talk to your parents about your concerns and their desires surrounding the upcoming birth and along with your husband, come to an agreement as to how much involvement you want them to have. One compromise is to have the expecting grandparents nearby but not actively involved. This way they can be invited into the birthing room immediately after the birth to share the first exciting moments with you. This offers them a more personal introduction to their new grandchild than just looking through a glass window. Being there, however, is the ultimate experience. If you invite your parents to share your baby's birth, they shouldn't pass up the opportunity. Their child is having a child. It is an important life event.

"My mother did not attend our baby's birth. She would have made me far too nervous," stated one mother. While another one says, "We already had a good relationship, but the experience made us even closer, perhaps because we now have shared that miracle of birth that only women can fully understand."

If it has been over twenty years since your parents were in a maternity ward, they probably realize that things have changed a lot. Perhaps your mother was sedated during your birth and has never actually seen a baby being born. Or if your parents had their children during the wild 70s, they may have had natural childbirth. But today's hospital birth is more mechanized than hospital births of the past and a delivering woman can look like she is in intensive care.

An Emotional Experience

It is no wonder some parents and grandparents are hesitant and find it hard to decide on who should share the birth. There are a lot of emotional issues involved. Many prospective grandparents feel that birthing is a private event and they shouldn't intrude. Many new parents feel the same way. But the birth experience, while being personal, is not a sexual experience. By the time you are in active labor and have been checked by numerous members of the hospital staff, having your mother or mother-in-law in the room will not seem like an invasion of privacy. Even expectant grandfathers, who swore they would remain outside the room, sometimes are caught up in the excitement and stay for the actual birth without embarrassment. Most of the invasion of privacy comes when eager fathers-to-be take videos that later few will be allowed to watch.

"I could not have done it without my mother. She was great; very strong and supportive. She anticipated all of my needs without hovering. She didn't let it show that she was worried or anything. She let the midwives and my husband run the show pretty much," reported new mother, Sheila.

Says Carol, a grandmother, "It demonstrated to me as nothing else ever could how much our daughters loved their father and me by being willing to share this most wonderful and private of experiences with us."

If you are having a hospital birth, your birth attendants, whether they are your parents, in-laws, or friends, need to have some preparation before the event. Even if a home birth is planned, education will benefit grandparents who wish to be present. You might suggest your mother attend the hospital tour with you and your husband, and that she meet your doctor before the big day. There are many books available to bring her up to date with birthing practices today and the equipment used. She will be more relaxed and better equipped to support you, if terms and procedures are familiar to her and she knows her way around the hospital. She needs to be rested, in good health, and have her own needs anticipated before she joins you at the birth, because no one will have time to attend to her.

A little preparation makes the event more comfortable for everyone present: the doctor, the expecting couple, the hospital staff or midwife, and the grandparents.

Relief for Husbands

One of the reasons for having grandparents present at the delivery is because they can relieve your husband of some of his chores. If he doesn't have to be the photographer, he can be more responsive and focused on your needs. In addition, this allows you both to be in the pictures with your new baby. And your mother or father will be more likely to take pictures that you can show others, unlike zealous husbands who find your nudity familiar.

During unattractive moments in childbirth, your mother may be of more help and be able to offer more specialized

A Grandmother in the Delivery Room

First-time grandmother Kelley Quinlivan, 58, of Fairfield [Connecticut] said her daughter, Sarah Etters, 27, of Derby, [Connecticut] asked her in advance to be in the delivery room when daughter Reesa Kathleen Etters was born on Sept. 27. "I think it was the most amazing experience I ever had. Both my children were Caesarians," said Quinlivan. "To be able to coach her and encourage her was just so special and then when the baby was born, it was an intense feeling of love and happiness. You couldn't believe this little miracle."

Eileen Fisher, "Who You Callin' Grandma,"
The Connecticut Post Online, April 14, 2008, www.connpost.com.

comfort than your husband is. She not only has known you longer than he has but she is a woman and has given birth herself. If you have a close relationship with her, you may want her near you. She has been the one to comfort you when you hurt in the past.

Husbands often feel helpless when you are in pain. They are scared and don't feel adequate no matter what they do. They can't empathize with you; they truly have never been through what you are going through. Many of them are in the room only because you insisted they be there; many of them faint. (I have never seen or heard of a grandmother fainting, however.) Your husband is an important person at the birth event, no doubt about it. He is there to love you, keep you company and be a support. He has a heavy and awesome responsibility. Ease some of his burden by letting your parent/s help out. They have an unconditional love for you and a thick skin. You won't be as likely to hurt their feelings if you yell at them during transition and there are some jobs they may be better equipped for than your husband, such as holding the tray while you throw up.

"I figured she was with me through puberty so she's seen me at my worst and if I got mean, she would probably be more understanding than my husband," stated one expecting mother.

"When I soiled myself in labor I was more comfortable with my mom cleaning me up than my husband. I mean, she had done that so many times before, granted I was slightly smaller then," said a new mom.

If things don't go as planned, you and your husband may need other support. Decisions can be daunting if the husband has to make them alone. An understanding and supportive family can be a great help if they are present when an emergency occurs.

Grandparents can be great attendants at your birth if they are welcome and prepared. As one new mother put it, "We have had grandmothers at every birth and even a grandfather, aunts, and other children. When they are properly trained in what your expectation is, it is a wonderful family event."

> *"These days, however, there is perhaps an even more excruciating experience [than childbirth]: having your mother in the delivery room."*

Grandmothers Are Not Helpful During Childbirth

Rebecca Eckler

Rebecca Eckler is the author of Knocked Up: Confessions of a Hip Mother-To-Be. *In the following viewpoint, she examines the recent trend of allowing grandmothers to be present in the delivery room. She argues that mothers and mothers-in-law can make labor and delivery more difficult for mothers-to-be because they are too emotionally involved. Even with the best of intentions, grandmothers can make expectant mothers anxious by not understanding their roles as caregivers and not medical practitioners. Eckler urges soon-to-be-moms to carefully consider whether they want their mothers present in the delivery room.*

As you read, consider the following questions:

1. On average, how many people are permitted in the delivery room in Canada, according to the viewpoint?

2. According to Dr. Collin Birch, what are the three main types of grandmothers who attend childbirths?

3. In addition to grandmothers, who are some other people Eckler lists that mothers-to-be have requested attend childbirth?

They say there is no greater pain than childbirth. These days, however, there is perhaps an even more excruciating experience: having your mother in the delivery room. "It was the worst decision I ever made," says Torontonian [Canada] Stacey Otis, 34, of having her mom there for the birth of her first child. "My mother kept walking in and out of the hospital room and pacing. Finally, I just yelled at her, 'Stay in or get out!' She stayed." When Otis's mother saw the baby's head, she fainted. "So my mother was lying on the floor and the doctor was yelling at me to yell at my mother that I was all right. So my baby wasn't even out, my doctor was screaming at me, I was screaming at my mother, 'I'm fine! I'm fine!' I just thought to myself, 'You've got to be kidding me!'"

Having your mother in the delivery room is "definitely a trend," says Dr. Colin Birch, a Calgary obstetrician. Dr. Paul Bernstein, an obstetrician in Toronto for 30 years, says he has even had mothers-in-law in the delivery room. "The mother-in-laws are great too because they can be more objective because it's not their child going through it." According to Birch, it has a lot to do with hospitals' more liberal views on the number of people permitted in the delivery room. Now, more often than not, at least two people can go in.

"I'd definitely say the hair on the back of my neck rises a bit every time I have a patient who asks if her mother can be in the room, or when I walk in and see their mother is present," Birch says. He tries, most of the time unsuccessfully, to discourage it. "I think it's a very private moment and I just don't understand it. But from my point of view, I know their mothers will be asking a thousand questions like, 'What's happening now? What are you doing?' Even though their daughters can be 30 years old, they start treating them like teenagers. My all-time favorite is when a mother says to me, 'My labour wasn't like this,' as if everyone has the same experience during childbirth. They forget what it's like."

Paula Couto, 38, of Toronto, also had a painful childbirth. And not only because she chose to go the natural route. "I wanted to walk around to get the baby to come out quicker. One of the nurses took me to the washroom and my mother was trailing behind us praying with her rosary beads. She started screaming, 'She's going to have the baby in the toilet! She's going to have the baby in the toilet!' My husband didn't know whether he should be calming me down or my mother. I thought he was going to strangle her." The experience got worse, says Couto. "When my mother saw the forceps, she really lost it and was screaming and praying so loud that everyone was staring at her." Few mothers can handle watching their children in pain. "We videotaped the labor and delivery," says Otis. "My mother just looked green the entire time."

Three Types of Mothers

According to Birch, there are three types of mothers who end up in the delivery room. "The first kind has a fixed idea of how they went through childbirth and they expect their daughters to have the same experience." The second kind "think they're being a good guardian, but for the most part, that's so far from the truth. They are a nuisance. They'd be more useful at home helping out after the baby is born. The third type are usually the mothers of single parents, because they're the woman's main support system."

Thirty-three-year-old Jasmine Miller, a single mother in Toronto, had her mom with her when she gave birth. "I couldn't have done it without her." While Miller wouldn't generally feel comfortable walking around naked in front of her mother, she would ask her to be with her again, should she

Grandma, Interrupted

"When a loved one invites you into that [delivery] room," says Cathy, a Florida grandmother of two, "it's one of the highest compliments the person could give you. If my daughter invited a stranger [like a doula] in lieu of me, my feelings would be hurt. I would secretly wonder why—is it because I would be too emotional? Is my relationship with her not close enough?"

While Cathy says she'd swallow the disappointment and accept her daughter's decision, she would wonder if a doula could have the unconditional love for the woman giving birth that a mother does.

Erin Meanley, "Dueling with the Doula,"
September 23, 2007, www.grandparent.com,.

have another child. In the process of giving birth, say most women, all modesty goes out the window. As Otis notes, "There were so many people looking at my vagina every 15 seconds, I didn't care what my mother saw."

Last year, Sherie Katz, 32, who lives in Toronto, asked her mother to be in the delivery room, along with her husband. "We're very close. And at all the prenatal classes, they basically tell you not to expect your husband to be your coach." And when Rena Wineberg, 43, arrived at a Toronto hospital in labor with her third child, her mother met her and her husband there. Fred Wineberg says he doesn't think he had "much choice" over his mother-in-law being in the room. "But I'd been there for the birth of three children before that. So I was like, 'Why not? Let's make this a party.'"

Birch worries that the trend will lead to even more people showing up. "Lately, I've even had people ask if their fathers could be in the room. And that I actively try to discourage. A lot of women, if they have other children, want the siblings in the room too. Pretty soon the entire extended family will be allowed in. What's next?" Some women agree with Birch. "My mother would be horrified to hear this, but I definitely wouldn't want her there," says Tara, a 33-year-old Calgary woman who had a baby last month. "I think she would just annoy me—and I would end up taking everything out on her first."

Periodical Bibliography

The following articles have been selected to supplement the diverse views presented in this chapter.

Donyale Abe	"Inclusive Childbirth Class," *International Journal of Childbirth Education*, vol. 22, no. 4, December 2007/January 2008.
Ellise D. Adams and Ann L. Bianchi	"A Practical Approach to Labor Support," *Journal of Obstetric, Gynecologic, and Neonatal Nursing*, vol. 37, no. 1, January/February 2008.
Steven A. Harvey et al.	"Are Skilled Birth Attendants Really Skilled? A Measurement Method, Some Disturbing Results and a Potential Way Forward," *World Health Organization. Bulletin of the World Health Organization*, vol. 85, no. 10, Oct 2007.
Erica Jorgensen	"Surrounded by Support," *Fit Pregnancy*, December 2007/January 2008.
Naunidhi Kaur	"Canada: Unassisted into the World," *Women's Feature Service*, September 25, 2007.
Kimberly N. Kline	"Midwife Attended Births in Prime-Time Television: Craziness, Controlling Bitches, and Ultimate Capitulation," *Women and Language*, Spring 2007.
Pamela Paul	"And the Doula Makes Four," *New York Times*, March 2, 2008.
Ziana Qaiser	"USA: Doulas: Birthing Women's Best Friend," *Women's Feature Service*, December 18, 2007.
Debby Takikawa	"The Business of Being a Birth Activist," *Mothering*, January/February 2008.
Carmen Germaine Warner	"Witness to a Miracle," *RN*, vol. 71, no. 2, February 2008.

For Further Discussion

Chapter 1

1. What evidence does Kathryn J. Alexander give for why epidurals are safe for the management of labor pain? What evidence does Sarah J. Buckley offer against the safety of epidurals? Whose viewpoint do you find most convincing, and why?

2. Gerard M. DiLeo advocates for the use of episiotomies during delivery on a case-by-case basis. Based on the evidence he provides, can you imagine circumstances in which episiotomies might be necessary? Do you agree with Beth Howard, who asserts that episiotomies are over-used and rarely necessary?

Chapter 2

1. Cynthia Overgard argues that women should be given ample choices for where they will give birth. Margaret McCartney asserts that giving women so many childbirth choices can lead to new mothers feeling less satisfied if their childbirth experience is not ideal. After reading these two viewpoints, how do you think choice impacts expectations about childbirth and the actual childbirth experience for women?

2. Janelle Weiner and Catherine Bennett debate the safety of home births. Which viewpoint offers the strongest evidence? Explain your answer.

3. William Caman and Kathyrn Alexander argue that hospital births are safe, while Yvonne Cryns argues that hospital births often involve unnecessary and unsafe procedures. Which viewpoint is more convincing? Why?

Chapter 3

1. Childbirth Connection discusses the rights that should be guaranteed to all childbearing women. How have other viewpoints in this chapter shaped your ideas about the rights and preferences of childbearing women?

2. Howard A. Janet argues that fetal monitors should be used during labor because they can reduce cerebral palsy risks. Michael F. Greene argues that fetal monitors are a hindrance to laboring women and do not lower the risks of cerebral palsy. Based on the evidence offered, do you think fetal monitors should be used during labor? Why or why not?

3. Judith Lothian argues that birth plans can improve women's perceptions of the childbirth experience, while Ingela Lundgren, Marie Berg, and Ginilla Lindmark argue that they do not. Based on these viewpoints, do you think pregnant women should write birth plans? Explain your answer.

4. What evidence does Mary E. Hannah use to argue that women should have the right to elective cesarean sections? What evidence do Kathi Carlisle Fountain and Kristen Suthers offer to argue that cesarean sections should not be routinely performed? Whose viewpoint is most convincing to you, and why?

Chapter 4

1. Kristen Davenport asserts that doulas can be helpful during childbirth, while Lucy Freeman argues that they are more of a hindrance to birthing women. Which viewpoint is more persuasive? Explain your answer.

2. Do you agree with Jon Marshall that midwives can be a positive part of the childbirth experience for some women. Why?

3. The Fatherhood Institute asserts the importance of fathers being present during childbirth, whereas Sandra Dick thinks they are more of a hindrance than a help. Which viewpoint is most convincing? Why?

4. Carolyn Bauer Zorn and Rebecca Eckler debate the presence of grandmothers in the delivery room. Based on the evidence offered, do you think grandmothers should be present at the births of their grandchildren?

Organizations to Contact

The editors have compiled the following list of organizations concerned with the issues debated in this book. The descriptions are derived from materials provided by the organizations. All have publications or information available for interested readers. The list was compiled on the date of publication of the present volume; the information provided here may change. Be aware that many organizations take several weeks or longer to respond to inquiries, so allow as much time as possible.

Association of Labor Assistants and Childbirth Educators (ALACE)
PO Box 390436, Cambridge, MA   02139
(888) 222-5223
e-mail: info@alace.org
Web site: www.alace.org

The Association of Labor Assistants and Childbirth Educators (ALACE) is an international nonprofit organization dedicated to supporting women's choices in childbirth. ALACE trains and certifies childbirth educators and labor assistants/birth doulas. In addition to offering position statements and other resources on their Web site, ALACE publishes a quarterly journal, *Special Delivery*.

American College of Obstetricians and Gynecologists (ACOG)
409 Twelfth Street SW, PO Box 96920
Washington, DC   20090-6920
(202) 638-5577
e-mail: resources@acog.org
Web site: www.acog.org

Founded in 1951 in Chicago, Illinois, the American College of Obstetricians and Gynecologists (ACOG) has over 52,000 members. Based in Washington, D.C., it is a private, voluntary, nonprofit membership organization that works primarily in four areas: serving as a strong advocate for quality health care for women, maintaining the highest standards of clinical practice and continuing education for its members, promoting patient education and stimulating patient understanding of and involvement in medical care, and increasing awareness among its members and the public of the changing issues facing women's health care. In addition to regularly posting position statements and patient information pamphlets on their Web site, ACOG publishes several journals including *Ethics in Obstetrics and Gynecology* and *Obstetrics and Gynecology (Green Journal)*.

American Pregnancy Association (APA)
1425 Greenway Drive, Suite 440, Irving, TX   75038
(972) 550-0140 • fax: (972) 550-0800
e-mail: Questions@AmericanPregnancy.org
Web site: www.americanpregnancy.org

The American Pregnancy Association (APA) is a national health organization committed to promoting reproductive and pregnancy wellness through education, research, advocacy, and community awareness. The APA seeks to support women and families by lobbying the legislature, businesses, and insurance providers to promote pregnancy and family health issues. In addition, by utilizing a toll-free helpline, the Internet, and patient education materials, the APA is able to deliver instant answers and provide access to resources on pregnancy topics, such as ectopic pregnancy, twin pregnancies, and gestational diabetes.

Association for Safe Alternatives to Childbirth (ASAC)
Main PO Box 1197, Edmonton, AB   T5J 2M4
   Canada
(780) 425-7993 • fax: (780) 497-7576
e-mail: info@asac.ab.ca
Web site: www.asac.ab.ca

The Association for Safe Alternatives to Childbirth (ASAC) was formed in 1979 as a consumer group concerned with choices in childbirth. After more than two decades, ASAC continues to be a strong organization, committed to parents in the community who are seeking support for their birthing and parenting choices. In addition to sponsoring regular lecture series', ASAC publishes *Birth Issues*, a quarterly magazine that emphasizes choice, awareness, and a natural, healthful approach to these topics.

Birth Network National

PO Box 2370, Birmingham, MI   48012
(888) 452-4784
e-mail: info@birthnetwork.org
Web site: www.birthnetwork.org

Birth Network National is a nonprofit organization that supports anyone seeking information, resources and support for safe, patient-directed maternity care. Guided by the "Mother-Friendly Childbirth Initiative" distributed by the Coalition for Improving Maternity Services, Birth Network engages in activism and legislative initiatives and provides resources for health care providers and expectant parents. In addition to position statements, their Web site offers many informational documents, including "Having a Baby? Ten Questions to Ask" and-"Midwifery Model of Care."

Childbirth Connection

281 Park Avenue S, 5th Floor, New York, NY   10010
(212) 777-5000 • fax: (212) 777-9320
Web site: www.childbirthconnection.org/

Founded in 1918, Childbirth Connection is a national not-for-profit organization dedicated to improving maternity care quality and value. They promote safe, effective, and satisfying evidence-based maternity care for women and families. The Childbirth Connection Web site offers a number of resources, including such publications as *Listening to Mothers II* and *A Guide to Effective Care in Pregnancy and Childbirth.*

Citizens for Midwifery (CfM)
PO Box 82227, Athens, GA   30608-2227
(888) 236-4880
e-mail: info@cfmidwifery.org
Web site: http://cfmidwifery.org/

Citizens for Midwifery (CfM) is a nonprofit, volunteer, grass-roots organization that was founded by several mothers in 1996. It promotes the Midwives Model of Care, which argues for the normalcy of birth and for the uniqueness of each childbearing woman and her family. CfM offers many online resources, including "Citizens for Midwifery" and "Safety of Home Birth: Planned Home Birth is Safe for Most Mothers and Babies."

Coalition for Improving Maternity Services (CIMS)
PO Box 2346, Ponte Vedra Beach, FL   32004
(888) 282-2467 • fax: (904) 285-2120
e-mail: info@motherfriendly.org
Web site: www.motherfriendly.org/

The Coalition for Improving Maternity Services (CIMS) is a coalition of individuals and organizations with concern for the care and well-being of mothers, babies, and families. Its mission is to promote a wellness model of maternity care that will improve birth outcomes and substantially reduce costs. CIMS offers numerous online resources, including publications such as "Are Your Birth Classes Mother-Friendly?" and "Fact Sheet: Problems and Hazards of Induction in Labor."

Doulas of North American (DONA) International
PO Box 626, Jasper, IN   47547
(888) 788-3662 • fax: (812) 634-1491
e-mail: Info@DONA.org
Web site: www.dona.org

Doulas of North American (DONA) International was founded in 1992 by a small group of foremost experts in childbirth. It is an organization that supports doulas who strive to help women and their partners to have satisfying childbirth and postpartum experiences. In addition to the quarterly journal, *International Doula*, DONA International regularly publishes position statements and research abstracts, many of which are available to nonmembers through its Web site.

International Childbirth Education Association (ICEA)
PO Box 20048, Minneapolis, MN   55420
(952) 854-8660 • fax: (952) 854-8772
e-mail: info@icea.org
Web site: www.icea.org

The International Childbirth Education Association (ICEA) is an organization of over four thousand members from throughout the United States and forty-two countries who believe in freedom of choice based on knowledge of alternatives in family-centered maternity and newborn care. ICEA offers a variety of learning opportunities for professional members and resources for expectant parents and new families. In addition to the quarterly publication of the *International Journal of Childbirth Education*, ICEA regularly issues position statements on childbirth issues, many of which can be found on its Web site.

Lamaze International
2025 M Street NW, Suite 800, Washington, DC   20036-3309
(800) 368-4404 • fax: (202) 367-2128
e-mail: education@lamaze.org
Web site: www.lamaze.org

The mission of Lamaze International is to promote, support and protect normal birth through education and advocacy. It believes that caregivers should respect the birth process and not intervene without compelling medical indication. In addition to position statements, the website provides a number of resources, including the journal *The Lamaze Institute for Normal Birth*.

Perinatal Education Associates (PEA)
98 E. Franklin Street, Suite B, Centerville, OH   45459
(866) 882-4784
Web site: www.birthsource.org

Perinatal Education Associates (PEA) is an international company dedicated to promoting positive pregnancy outcomes through education, promotion of evidence-based research, family centered care, maternal/child health advocacy and awareness. PEA offers health care professionals and expectant and new parents up-to-date information on pregnancy and childbirth. Through their Web site, they provide a library of articles, including "Epidural's Impact on Birth" and "Helpful Positions for Labor."

Bibliography of Books

Penny Armstrong, Sheryl Feldman, and Sheila Kitzinger
A Wise Birth: Bringing Together the Best of Natural Childbirth and Modern Medicine. London: Pinter and Martin, 2007.

Elisabeth A. Aron
Pregnancy Dos and Don'ts: The Smart Woman's Pocket Companion for a Safe and Sound Pregnancy. New York: Broadway Books, 2006.

Jacky Bloemraad-De Boer
A–Z For a Healthy Pregnancy and Natural Childbirth. London: Author House, 2007.

Robert A. Bradley, Marjie Hathaway, Jay Hathaway, and James Hathaway
Husband-Coached Childbirth: The Bradley Method of Natural Childbirth. 5th ed. New York: Bantam, May 2008.

Phyllis L. Brodsky
The Control of Childbirth: Women Versus Medicine Through the Ages. Jefferson, NC: McFarland, 2008.

Jane Buckingham
The Modern Girl's Guide to Motherhood. New York: Reagan Books, 2006.

Dori Hillestad Butler and Carol Thompson
My Mom's Having a Baby! Morton Grove, IL: Albert Whitman & Company, 2005.

Sheldon H. Cherry and Douglas G. Moss
Understanding Pregnancy and Childbirth. 4th ed. Hoboken, NJ: John Wiley and Sons, 2004.

Deepak Chopra, David Simon, and Vicki Abrams — *Magical Beginnings, Enchanted Lives: A Holistic Guide to Pregnancy and Childbirth*. New York: Three Rivers Press, 2005.

Marisa Cohen — *Deliver This!: Make the Childbirth Choice That's Right for You . . . No Matter What Everyone Else Thinks*. Jackson, TN: Seal Press, 2007.

Michael R. Crider — *The Guy's Guide to Surviving Pregnancy, Childbirth, and the First Year of Fatherhood*. Cambridge, MA: Da Capo Press, 2005.

Gail J. Dahl — *Pregnancy and Childbirth Secrets*. Louisville, KY: Innovative Publishing, 2007.

Grantly Dick-Read — *Childbirth Without Fear: The Principles and Practice of Natural Childbirth*. 4th ed. London: Pinter and Martin, 2004.

Deirdre Dolan and Alexandra Zissu — *The Complete Organic Pregnancy*. New York: Collins, 2006.

Ann Douglas and John R. Sussman — *The Unofficial Guide to Having a Baby*. 2nd ed. New York, NY: Wiley, 2004.

Sheila Kitzinger — *The Politics of Birth*. New York: Elsevier Butterworth Heinemann, 2005.

Erica Lyon — *The Big Book of Birth*. New York: Plume Book, 2007.

Sheri Menelli	*Journey into Motherhood: Inspirational Stories of Natural Birth.* Encinitas, CA: White Heart Publishing, 2004.
Michele C. Moore and Caroline M. deCosta	*Pregnancy and Parenting After Thirty-Five: Mid Life, New Life.* Baltimore, MD: Johns Hopkins University Press, 2006.
Rebecca Odes	*From the Hips: A Comprehensive, Open-Minded, Uncensored, Totally Honest Guide to Pregnancy, Birth, and Becoming a Parent.* New York: Three Rivers Press, 2007.
Richard K. Reed	*Birthing Fathers: The Transformation of Men in American Rites of Birth.* New Brunswick, NJ: Rutgers University Press, 2005.
Laura Riley	*Pregnancy: The Ultimate Week-by-Week Pregnancy Guide.* Des Moines, IA: Meredith Books, 2006.
Janet Schwegel, ed.	*Adventures in Natural Childbirth: Tales from Women on the Joys, Fears, Pleasures, and Pains of Giving Birth Naturally.* New York: Marlowe, 2005.
Penny Simkin	*The Birth Partner: A Complete Guide to Childbirth for Dads, Doulas, and Other Labor Companions.* 3rd ed. Boston, MA: Harvard Common Press, 2008.
Amy L. Sutton	*Pregnancy and Birth Sourcebook.* 2nd ed. Detroit, MI: Omnigraphics, 2004.

Giuditta Tornetta   *Painless Childbirth: An Empowering Journey Through Pregnancy and Childbirth.* Nashville, TN: Cumberland House Publishing, 2008.

Marsden Wagner   *Born in the USA: How a Broken Maternity System Must Be Fixed to Put Women and Children First.* Berkeley: University of California Press, 2006.

Index